THE BIG BOOK OF MIXOLOGY
5 IN 1

The Ultimate Guide for Beginners to Craft Classic, Tiki and Smoked Cocktails to Become The Perfect Home Bartender

Chris Doherty

© Copyright 2023 by Chris Doherty - All rights reserved.

All rights reserved. No part of this book may be reproduced in any form without permission in writing from the author. Reviewers may quote brief passages in reviews.

While all attempts have been made to verify the information provided in this publication, neither the author nor the publisher assumes any responsibility for errors, omissions, or contrary interpretation of the subject matter herein.

The views expressed in this publication are those of the author alone and should not be taken as expert instruction or commands. The reader is responsible for his or her own actions, as well as his or her own interpretation of the material found within this publication.

Adherence to all applicable laws and regulations, including international, federal, state and local governing professional licensing, business practices, advertising, and all other aspects of doing business in the US, Canada or any other jurisdiction is the sole responsibility of the reader and consumer.

Neither the author nor the publisher assumes any responsibility or liability whatsoever on behalf of the consumer or reader of this material. Any perceived slight of any individual or organization is purely unintentional.

Table of Contents

FOREWORD 11
BOOK 1 12
THE ART OF MIXOLOGY 12
INTRODUCTION 13
MIXOLOGY 101 14
    what is mixology? 14
    History of mixology 15
    MIXOLOGY IN THE MODERN ERA 16
    Mixologist vs. Bartender 17

BASIC BUILDING BLOCKS OF MIXOLOGY 19
    Liquor 19
    Mixers 20
    Garnishes 20
    Ice 20
    Glassware 21

THE MIXOLOGY TECHNIQUES 22
    Different techniques for mixing drinks 22
    Principles of dilution, ice & temperature 24
    Importance of presentation & garnishing 25
    Presentation Techniques 26

Classic Cocktails 29
    History and Evolution of Classic Cocktails 29
    Essential Ingredients & Techniques 31
    Tips for creating perfect classic cocktails 32

Modern Cocktails 35
    Importance of experimentation 35

- Modern twists on classic cocktails 36
- Modern Twists Examples 37
- Creation of new and innovative drinks 39
- Modern Twists on the Creation of Innovative Drinks Examples 40
- How to start creating new variations 42

Advanced Mixology Techniques 44

- Molecular mixology techniques & tools 44
- custom syrups, bitters & tinctures 47
- Advanced techniques for impressive drinks 50

Responsible Mixology 52

- Social responsibility in the drinking industry 52
- Low-Alcohol & Alcohol-Free Cocktails 54
- Importance of responsible service and consumption 56

CONCLUSION 59

BOOK 2 61

INTRODUCTION 62

Some Theory 63

- History of Classic Cocktails 63
- What makes a Cocktail Classic? 65
- Why classic cocktails are still popular 66

THE CLASSICS 68

- Old Fashioned 68
- Martini 69
- Manhattan 70
- Negroni 70
- Sazerac 71
- Daiquiri 72
- Margarita 73
- Sidecar 73
- Gin & Tonic 74

Whiskey Sour 75

Whiskey Sour 76

The Evolution of Classic Cocktails 77

Modern twists on classic recipes 78

Using unique ingredients and techniques 79

The future of classic cocktails 81

CONCLUSION 83

BOOK 3 84

SMOKED COCKTAILS 84

INTRODUCTION 85

SMOKED COCKTAILS 101 87

History of Smoked Cocktails 87

Regional Variations 89

Classic Smoked Cocktails 91

MODERN INTERPRETATIONS 92

The Science Behind Smoke-Infused Flavors 94

The Chemistry of Smoke and Alcohol 94

The Impact of Wood on Flavor and Aroma 95

Different Types of Wood and Their Characteristics 97

Smoking Techniques & Their Effects 99

Combining flavors with smoke 101

Smoking Techniques 104

Using a Handheld Smoker 105

Using a Smoke Box 106

Smoking with Wood Chips 107

Smoking with Herbs & Spices 109

Safety Precautions for Smoking Cocktails 111

The Art of Smoked Cocktails 113

Selecting the right glassware 113

Choosing the Right Garnishes 115

Understanding the Importance of Ice 116

Stirring Vs. Shaking 117

Sipping vs. shooting 119

Pairing Smoked Cocktails with Food 122

Understanding the flavor profile of smoked cocktails 122

Pairing Smoked Cocktails with Appetizers 124

Pairing smoked cocktails with entrees 125

Pairing smoked cocktails with desserts 127

CONCLUSION 129

BOOK 4 130

TIKI DRINKS 130

INTRODUCTION 131

MYSTERIES OF AN ANCIENT CIVILIZATION 133

Birth Of New Populations 133

Colonization 134

Tribal Peoples 134

Tiki art and history 135

Marquesas Islands & Meaning of Tiki 136

THE TIKI CULTURE 137

The success of the Tiki Culture 137

Expanding Tiki Culture 138

The decline of Tiki culture 139

Difference between Tiki and Tropical 140

1st Reason: Tiki Bars 140

2nd Reason: Tropical Fruit & Rum 140

3rd Reason: Tropical Influences On Tiki 141

TIKI MIXING: VARIATIONS BETWEEN ERAS 144

What is meant by Tiki mixing? 144

The Birth Of Tiki// The First Era 146

Evolution of Cocktails// The Second Era 147
Parallel Tiki mixing 149
The Contamination Of Classics With Tiki Mixing 151

TIKI MUG: JUST MARKETING? 153

From the first exotic Tiki Bar to the Tiki Mug 153
The First Tiki Glasses 153
Birth and diffusion of the Tiki Mug 154
Trader Vic and the Tiki Mugs 155
Art and fantasy in Tiki Bars 156

HOW TO MAKE TIKI COCKTAIL TWISTS 159

The Twists of Tiki Cocktails 159
Traditional Approach 160
The Conceptual Value Of Tiki 162
Tips for Tiki Cocktail Twists 164

TIKI COCKTAIL INGREDIENTS 166

Understanding TIKI Cocktails To Twist Them 168
Sample Processing Of Tiki Cocktail Ingredients 169

TIKI COCKTAIL TWISTS EXAMPLES 172

First Example: Don's Special Daiquiri 172
Second Example: Missionary's Downfall 174
Third Example: The Zombie 176

BOOK 5 180

COCKTAIL RECIPES 180

CLASSIC RECIPES 181

Blackberry Mint Julep 181
Maple Old Fashioned 182
Grapefruit Negroni 183
Lavender Lemon Drop 183
Spiced Manhattan 184
Gingerbread Old Fashioned 185

Espresso Martini 185

Rosemary Gin Fizz 186

Honey Sage Margarita 187

Cinnamon Hot Toddy 187

Cherry Amaretto Sour 188

SMOKED RECIPES **189**

Smoked Whiskey Sour 189

Smoky Margarita 190

Smoke & Mirrors 191

Smoked Maple Old Fashioned 192

Smoked Chocolate Martini 193

Smoked Grapefruit Margarita 193

Smoked Pineapple Margarita 194

Smoky Manhattan 195

Smoked Bloody Mary 196

Smoky Espresso Martini 197

Smoked Cherry Manhattan 198

Smoked Grapefruit Paloma 199

TIKI RECIPES **201**

Missionary's Downfall 201

Eastern Sour Cocktail 202

Navy Grog Cocktail 203

Don's Special Daiquiri 204

Scorpion Cocktail 205

Forbidden Mai Tai 206

The Authentic Mai Tai 207

Zombie 207

Sweet Painkiller 208

BLUE HAWAIIAN 209

Bahama Mama 210

FOREWORD

Welcome to the world of mixology, where creativity, passion, and precision meet to create masterful cocktails. In this book, you will embark on a journey through the history, techniques, and all the secrets. Whether you're an experienced bartender or an enthusiastic amateur, this book will take you on a fascinating ride through the world of cocktails.

Mixology is an art that requires both technical skills and imagination. It's not just about pouring a drink or shaking a cocktail shaker. It's about creating an experience for the senses, an explosion of flavors, aromas, and colors that leave a lasting impression. And in this book, you will discover how to do just that.

Starting with the history, you will learn how cocktails evolved from their early days as medicinal tonics to the sophisticated and complex drinks we enjoy today. You'll explore the role of famous bartenders, the birth of classic cocktails, and the trends that have shaped the cocktail culture over time.

But mixology is not just about the past. It's also about the present and the future. And in this book, you'll discover the latest techniques and trends that are pushing the boundaries of this world. From molecular mixology to fusion cocktails, you'll learn how to incorporate new techniques and ingredients to create exciting new drinks that surprise and delight.

Of course, to create masterful cocktails, you need to have a strong foundation in the techniques of mixology. In this book, you will learn the basics of mixing drinks, from measuring and shaking to stirring and straining. You'll also learn the art of garnishing, which can transform a simple drink into a stunning work of art.

You'll learn how to combine flavors and ingredients, how to balance sweet and sour, and how to add a touch of flair and personality to every drink you make. So, are you ready to explore the world of mixology? To learn the history, the techniques, and the secrets of this fascinating art? To unleash your creativity and craft cocktails that amaze and delight? Then join us on this journey, and let's raise a glass to the world of cocktails!

BOOK 1

THE ART OF MIXOLOGY

INTRODUCTION

Are you tired of the same old boring drinks? Do you want to impress your friends and family with unique and delicious cocktails? Look no further than the world of mixology! In this book, you will discover the secrets of creating amazing cocktails that are sure to dazzle and delight. Whether you're a seasoned bartender or a curious amateur, there's something for everyone in the world of mixology.

We'll start by exploring the basic building blocks of mixology, from the different types of liquor to the techniques for mixing them. You'll learn the difference between shaken and stirred drinks, how to properly muddle ingredients, and the essential tools every mixologist needs in their arsenal.

But mixology is more than just technique; it's also an art form. In this book, we'll explore the creative side of mixology, including the use of unique ingredients, the creation of custom syrups and bitters, and the art of garnishing. You'll learn how to incorporate unexpected flavors like herbs and spices, how to create visually stunning drinks that are as beautiful as they are delicious, and how to put your own unique spin on classic cocktails. And if you're feeling particularly adventurous, we'll even explore the world of molecular mixology. From foams and gels to dry ice and liquid nitrogen, we'll show you how to take your mixology game to the next level.

But perhaps most importantly, we'll show you how to have fun while you're mixing drinks. Mixology is about experimentation, exploration, and above all, enjoyment. So grab your shaker, your favorite liquor, and a sense of adventure, and let's dive into this exciting world!

MIXOLOGY 101

If you've ever been to a cocktail bar or a trendy club, you've surely had the chance to order your favorite cocktail: a negroni, a margarita, a cosmopolitan... when it comes to cocktails, you're really spoiled for choice! But not everyone knows that mixology is an art that has evolved only in the last few decades, and is now all the rage in trendy clubs.

WHAT IS MIXOLOGY?

Mixology is the art and science of creating cocktails. It involves the careful blending of different ingredients to create unique, flavorful, and aesthetically pleasing drinks. Mixology is not just about pouring drinks; it is about crafting an experience for the senses, combining flavors, textures, and colors to create a masterpiece in a glass.

The term mixology comes from the word "mixing," which refers to the act of combining different ingredients together. In the context of cocktails, mixology is the process of combining spirits, juices, syrups, and other ingredients to create a perfectly balanced drink. It is a highly skilled and creative profession that requires a deep knowledge of ingredients, techniques, and trends.

HISTORY OF MIXOLOGY

The art of creating drinks certainly has very ancient roots: since ancient times, humans have loved to invent drinks of all kinds, from wine mixed with spices and flavorings to early versions of beer. During the time of the ancient Romans, for example, the wine produced was really very strong and concentrated, and therefore had to be diluted: thus many variations of the "nectar of the gods" were born, with ingredients such as honey, cloves, saffron, fruit, and many others.

However, mixology as we understand it today was born after the industrial revolution, with the birth of masterfully created liqueurs and spirits. From the nineteenth century real cocktails began to emerge: the first concept of a "cocktail" originated in Great Britain, and it was similar to a punch, with fruit juices and spices. The actual term is defined in 1806 in New York, when the newspaper "The Balance and Columbian Repository" states that a cocktail is "*a liquor with a stimulating composition of any kind of sugar, water and bitters, vulgarly called bittered sling.*"

In 1862 it was Jerry Thomas (called "Professor" Thomas), a skilled American bartender born in Connecticut, who finally wrote the first cocktail recipe book, "The Bartender's Guide," a useful encyclopedia of mixed drinks. With the arrival of industrially produced ice, cocktails also evolved, until the coming of Prohibition in America, which slowed down the consumption of alcohol but did not completely stop its advance. After World War II, American-born cocktails fell under the spell of foreign countries, evolving even more; in the 20th century, however, some of the still most famous cocktails, such as the Manhattan or the Martini, were born.

To this day, the art of mixology is increasingly famous and evolved, so much so that the classic bartender can evolve into the more refined mixologist: an artist of alcoholic beverages capable of recreating classics and reinventing ever more unique cocktails. A further addition to this profession is flair mixology, a complex of acrobatic techniques used to prepare drinks; these techniques, which are quite complicated and often difficult to master, include bottle flips, pouring multiple drinks at once, and much more. Flair mixology must never, however, lose sight of the quality and goodness of the cocktail it prepares in order to prioritize the acrobatic spectacle. Although more recent, flair mixology also has great popularity, and this technique also owes its birth to the great bartender Jerry Thomas.

MIXOLOGY IN THE MODERN ERA

Mixology has come a long way since the days of the traditional cocktail bar. Today, mixology is used in a variety of settings, from high-end restaurants to private events. Mixologists are not just creating new cocktails but are also experimenting with new techniques and ingredients to create unique and innovative drinks.

One of the most significant changes in the world of mixology has been the shift towards artisanal cocktails. In the past, cocktails were often made using pre-made mixes and standardized ingredients. Today, mixologists are focused on creating custom ingredients, including house-made syrups, bitters, and tinctures. This focus on artisanal ingredients has helped to elevate the quality of cocktails and has made mixology more of an art form than ever before.

Another trend in modern mixology is the use of unexpected ingredients. Mixologists are now experimenting with a wide range of ingredients, from herbs and spices to fruits, vegetables, and even savory elements. This experimentation has led to the creation of unique and surprising drinks that are designed to tantalize the senses.

Molecular mixology is another trend that has gained popularity in recent years. This technique involves using science to create new textures and flavors in cocktails. Techniques such as foams, gels, and liquid nitrogen are used to create drinks that are visually stunning and delicious.

Mixology is not just limited to bars and restaurants. It is now being used in a variety of settings, including weddings, corporate events, and private parties. Mixologists are being hired to create custom drinks that are tailored to the specific tastes and preferences of the event's attendees.

One of the most significant benefits of mixology is its ability to elevate the drinking experience. Mixologists are not just focused on creating a great-tasting drink, but they are also focused on the overall experience of the cocktail. From the presentation to the glassware, every element is carefully considered to create a memorable and enjoyable experience. Mixology is also being used to promote social responsibility in the drinking industry. Many mixologists are now focused on creating low-alcohol or alcohol-free cocktails, which offer a healthier and more responsible option for those who do not want to consume alcohol.

MIXOLOGIST VS. BARTENDER

While the terms mixologist and bartender are often used interchangeably, they are not the same thing. There are distinct differences between the two roles, and understanding these differences is important for anyone who is interested in the world of cocktails and mixology. At its core, bartending is a service industry. Bartenders are responsible for serving drinks to customers, taking orders, and ensuring that everyone has a great experience. Bartenders are typically found in bars, restaurants, and other venues where alcoholic beverages are served.

A mixologist, on the other hand, is someone who specializes in creating cocktails. Mixologists are experts in the art and science of mixology, and they are focused on creating unique and innovative drinks that are tailored to the tastes and preferences of their customers. While bartenders may also be skilled in mixology, they are not necessarily experts in the field. A bartender's primary responsibility is to serve drinks to customers, while a mixologist's primary responsibility is to create new and exciting drinks that push the boundaries of mixology.

Another key difference between a mixologist and a bartender is their level of training and expertise. Bartenders may receive some basic training in mixology as part of their job, but they are not typically required to have a deep understanding of the techniques and principles of mixology.

Mixologists, on the other hand, are highly trained professionals who have dedicated themselves to the art and science of mixology. They have a deep understanding of the different types of liquor, flavor profiles, and techniques involved in mixing drinks. They may also be trained in other areas, such as molecular mixology, which involves using science to create new textures and flavors in cocktails. Mixologists also tend to work in different settings than bartenders. While bartenders are primarily found in bars and restaurants, mixologists may work in a variety of settings, including high-end restaurants, hotels, and private events. Mixologists are often hired to create custom drinks that are tailored to the tastes and preferences of the event's attendees.

In conclusion, while the terms mixologist and bartender are often used interchangeably, they are not the same thing. Bartenders are responsible for serving drinks to customers, while mixologists are experts in the art and science of mixology, focused on creating unique and innovative drinks. Mixologists receive extensive training in mixology and may work in a variety of settings, including high-end restaurants and private events. Understanding the difference between these two roles is important for anyone who is interested in the world of cocktails and mixology.

BASIC BUILDING BLOCKS OF MIXOLOGY

Mixology is a complex and multifaceted art form that requires a deep understanding of the basic building blocks of cocktails. These building blocks are the foundation of all great cocktails, and they include liquor, mixers, and garnishes. In this chapter, we'll explore these building blocks in detail and provide practical tips and realistic advice for using them to create great cocktails.

LIQUOR

Liquor is the base of all cocktails and provides the alcohol content. There are many different types of liquor, including vodka, gin, rum, tequila, and whiskey, each with its own distinct flavor profile. When selecting liquor for a cocktail, it's important to consider the flavor of the liquor and how it will interact with the other ingredients in the drink.

Tip: When creating a cocktail, start with a quality base liquor. Look for high-quality spirits that are made from quality ingredients and distilled multiple times for a smooth taste.

MIXERS

Mixers are the non-alcoholic components of a cocktail and include juices, sodas, syrups, and bitters. Mixers are used to balance the flavor of the liquor and can add sweetness, sourness, bitterness, or complexity to the cocktail.

Tip: Experiment with different types of mixers to find the perfect balance for your cocktail. Start with a small amount of mixer and adjust to taste. Use fresh ingredients whenever possible, as they will add more flavor and complexity to the cocktail.

GARNISHES

Garnishes are the final touch that adds a visual and aromatic element to the cocktail. They are used to enhance the flavor of the cocktail and can add texture, color, and aroma.

Tip: When selecting a garnish, consider the flavors and aromas of the cocktail. Citrus peels are a great garnish for many cocktails, as they add a bright citrus flavor and aroma. Fresh herbs and spices can also be used to add complexity and depth to the cocktail.

ICE

Ice is a critical component of any cocktail, as it helps to dilute the liquor and create a balanced flavor profile. Different types of ice can be used for different cocktails, and it's important to consider the size, shape, and texture of the ice when selecting it for a drink.

Tip: Use high-quality ice that is free from impurities and has a clean taste. For cocktails that require a lot of ice, consider using a large block of ice that will melt slowly and create a consistent dilution.

GLASSWARE

The type of glassware used for a cocktail can have a significant impact on its flavor and presentation. Different types of glassware can enhance the aroma and taste of a cocktail and can create a unique and memorable drinking experience.

Tip: Choose glassware that is appropriate for the type of cocktail being served. For example, a martini is traditionally served in a martini glass, while a whiskey sour is served in a lowball glass. Use high-quality glassware that is clean and free from scratches or blemishes.

In conclusion, understanding the basic building blocks of mixology is essential for creating great cocktails. Liquor, mixers, garnishes, ice, and glassware are all critical components of a well-crafted cocktail. Experiment with different ingredients and techniques to create unique and innovative drinks that are tailored to your taste preferences. Remember to use high-quality ingredients, fresh garnishes, and appropriate glassware to create a memorable and enjoyable drinking experience.

THE MIXOLOGY TECHNIQUES

Mixology is as much a science as it is an art. The techniques used to mix cocktails are essential to achieving the perfect balance of flavors, textures, and aromas in a drink. In this chapter, we'll explore the different techniques used in mixology and provide practical tips and advice for mastering them. Whether you're a seasoned mixologist or a beginner, understanding these techniques will help you take your cocktail game to the next level. So, let's dive into the world of mixology and discover the techniques that make it an art form like no other.

DIFFERENT TECHNIQUES FOR MIXING DRINKS

Mixing drinks is an essential part of mixology, and there are several different techniques that mixologists use to create perfect cocktails. These techniques are critical to achieving the right balance of flavors, aromas, and textures in a drink. In this chapter, we'll explore some of the most common techniques for mixing drinks and provide practical tips for mastering them.

Shaking

Shaking is a common technique for mixing cocktails that include juice, cream, or egg whites. The technique involves adding the ingredients to a shaker with ice and shaking vigorously to create a frothy and well-mixed drink.

Tip: When shaking a cocktail, make sure to use a shaker that can hold enough ice to properly chill the drink. Shake the cocktail for at least 15 seconds to ensure that the ingredients are well mixed.

Stirring

Stirring is a technique that is used for cocktails that contain only liquor, such as a martini or Manhattan. The technique involves stirring the ingredients in a mixing glass with ice to create a well-mixed and perfectly chilled drink.

Tip: When stirring a cocktail, use a long-handled bar spoon to stir the ingredients in a circular motion. Stir the cocktail for at least 30 seconds to ensure that the ingredients are well mixed and chilled.

Muddling

Muddling is a technique that is used to release the flavors and aromas of fresh herbs, fruits, and spices. The technique involves crushing the ingredients in a mixing glass or shaker with a muddler to release their essential oils.

Tip: When muddling ingredients, be careful not to over-muddle or crush them too much, as this can release bitter or unwanted flavors. Use a gentle touch to release the essential oils and flavors of the ingredients.

Blending

Blending is a technique that is used to create frozen or blended drinks. The technique involves blending the ingredients in a blender with ice to create a smooth and well-mixed drink.

Tip: When blending a cocktail, make sure to use enough ice to create a thick and creamy texture. Start by blending the ingredients on low speed and gradually increase to high speed for a perfectly blended drink.

Building

Building is a technique that is used to create simple cocktails, such as a gin and tonic or a whiskey sour. The technique involves adding the ingredients to a glass and stirring to mix them together.

Tip: When building a cocktail, start by adding the base liquor to the glass and then add the mixer or other ingredients. Stir the cocktail gently to mix the ingredients together.

PRINCIPLES OF DILUTION, ICE & TEMPERATURE

The principles of dilution, ice, and temperature are critical components of mixology. These principles play a crucial role in achieving the perfect balance of flavors, aromas, and textures in a drink. In this chapter, we'll explore these principles in detail and provide practical tips and advice for using them to create perfect cocktails.

Dilution

Dilution is the process of adding water to a cocktail to lower its alcohol content and create a well-balanced and easy-to-drink cocktail. Dilution is achieved through the melting of ice, which adds a small amount of water to the drink.

Ice

Ice is a critical component of any cocktail, as it helps to chill and dilute the drink. Different types of ice can be used for different cocktails, and it's important to consider the size, shape, and texture of the ice when selecting it for a drink.

Temperature

Temperature is another critical component of mixology. The temperature of a drink can impact its flavor and texture, and it's important to consider the temperature of the ingredients and the glassware when creating a cocktail.

Experiment with different types of ice and consider the temperature of the ingredients and the glassware to create a perfectly chilled and well-balanced drink. Remember to use high-quality ice and chill the glassware to keep the drink cool and refreshing. These principles may seem simple, but mastering them takes practice and patience, and with the right tools and techniques, anyone can become a skilled mixologist.

IMPORTANCE OF PRESENTATION & GARNISHING

Presentation and garnishing are essential components of mixology that can elevate a drink from good to great and create a memorable drinking experience. In this chapter, we'll explore the importance of presentation and garnishing in mixology and provide practical tips and advice for creating beautiful and impressive cocktails.

The presentation of a drink is the first thing that a customer sees and can impact their perception of the drink before they even take a sip. Garnishing can add visual interest, texture, and flavor to a drink, creating a unique and memorable experience for the drinker. Consider the colors, textures, and shapes of the ingredients, and how they can be used to create a visually stunning drink.

Choosing the Right Glassware

The choice of glassware is another important factor in the presentation of a drink. Different types of glassware can enhance the aroma and taste of a cocktail and can create a unique and memorable drinking experience. Choose glassware that is appropriate for the type of cocktail being served. For example, a martini is traditionally served in a martini glass, while a whiskey sour is served in a lowball glass. Use high-quality glassware that is clean and free from scratches or blemishes.

Garnishing Techniques

There are several different techniques that can be used for garnishing cocktails, including using fruit peels, herbs, and spices. These ingredients can add flavor, aroma, and texture to a drink, creating a unique and memorable drinking experience. Experiment with different garnishing techniques to find the perfect garnish for your cocktail. Use fresh ingredients whenever possible, as they will add more flavor and complexity to the cocktail.

PRESENTATION TECHNIQUES

There are several different presentation techniques that can be used to create visually stunning cocktails, including layering, rimming, and using edible flowers. Take time to consider the presentation of your drink. Consider the colors, textures, and shapes of the ingredients, and how they can be used to create a visually stunning drink. Use a variety of techniques to create a drink that is not only delicious but also visually appealing.

Layering

Layering is a technique that involves creating distinct layers of different colored liquids in a cocktail. This technique can be used to create visually stunning drinks that are as beautiful as they are delicious.

- **Step 1:** Choose a glass that is appropriate for layering. Tall, narrow glasses work best for layering, as they allow the layers to be more distinct.
- **Step 2:** Start by pouring the heaviest and most viscous ingredient into the glass. This will typically be a syrup or liqueur.
- **Step 3:** Gently pour the next heaviest ingredient onto the back of a spoon and let it trickle down the sides of the glass. Repeat this process for each layer.
- **Step 4:** Finish the cocktail with a garnish that complements the colors of the layers. Citrus peels and fresh herbs work well for this.

Rimming

Rimming is a technique that involves coating the rim of a glass with a flavorful substance, such as salt or sugar. This technique can add texture and flavor to a cocktail and create a unique and memorable drinking experience.

- **Step 1:** Choose an appropriate glass. Wide-mouthed glasses work best for rimming, as they allow the rim to be coated evenly.
- **Step 2:** Prepare the coating by mixing a small amount of salt, sugar, or other flavorful substance with water or citrus juice.
- **Step 3:** Dip the rim of the glass into the coating mixture, making sure to coat the entire rim evenly.
- **Step 4:** Fill the glass with the cocktail, making sure not to disturb the rim. Add a garnish that complements the flavor of the coating.

Using Edible Flowers

Edible flowers can add a unique and visually stunning element to a cocktail. There are many different types of edible flowers that can be used for garnishing, including roses, pansies, and violets.

- **Step 1:** Choose a cocktail that would benefit from the addition of an edible flower. Cocktails with floral or fruity flavors work best for this.
- **Step 2:** Choose an edible flower that complements the flavor of the cocktail. The flower should be fresh and free from blemishes or insect damage.
- **Step 3:** Place the flower on top of the cocktail or skewer it with a cocktail pick.
- **Step 4:** Serve the cocktail immediately, making sure not to disturb the flower.

Take time to consider the presentation of your drink and experiment with different garnishing and presentation techniques to create a drink that is not only delicious but also visually stunning. Remember to use high-quality ingredients, fresh garnishes, and appropriate glassware to create a memorable and enjoyable drinking experience.

Classic Cocktails

Classic cocktails are timeless and have stood the test of time in the world of mixology. These cocktails have been enjoyed for decades and have become staples in the bar scene. We'll explore some of the most iconic classic cocktails and provide insight into their history, ingredients, and preparation. Whether you're a seasoned mixologist or a beginner, learning about classic cocktails can enhance your knowledge and appreciation of the art of mixology. So, let's dive into the world of classic cocktails and discover some of the most beloved and enduring drinks of all time.

HISTORY AND EVOLUTION OF CLASSIC COCKTAILS

Classic cocktails have a rich and fascinating history that has evolved over time. These timeless drinks have been enjoyed for decades, and their popularity continues to grow in the modern-day mixology scene. Understanding the history and evolution of classic cocktails can help you appreciate their origins, the cultural and social influences that shaped them, and their lasting legacy in the world of mixology.

Origins of Classic Cocktails

The origins of classic cocktails date back to the early 1800s, when bartending was considered an art form. Bartenders were creating cocktails to showcase their skills and creativity, and these drinks quickly became popular among patrons. The first known cocktail was the Sazerac, created in New Orleans in the 1830s, and its popularity led to the creation of other classic cocktails such as the Old Fashioned, the Martini, and the Manhattan.

As bartenders gained more experience, they began to experiment with new ingredients and techniques, leading to the creation of new and innovative drinks. Classic cocktails were a prominent feature in many social events, including parties, weddings, and even political rallies.

Prohibition and the Golden Age of Cocktails

Prohibition, which lasted from 1920 to 1933, drove cocktails underground and led to the rise of speakeasies. During this time, bartenders were forced to become more creative with their ingredients, as they often had limited access to high-quality spirits. This period also saw the rise of classic cocktails such as the Sidecar, the Daiquiri, and the Margarita, which have remained popular to this day.

After the repeal of Prohibition, the Golden Age of Cocktails began, which lasted until the 1950s. During this time, bartenders became more experimental and creative with their cocktails, using exotic ingredients such as fruits, herbs, and spices. Classic cocktails such as the Bloody Mary, the Mai Tai, and the Piña Colada were created during this period and remain popular today.

Modern-Day Adaptations

Classic cocktails have continued to evolve over the years, with mixologists adding new twists and variations to the original recipes. Some bartenders have even created their own unique cocktails that pay homage to the classics while adding their own unique twist.

In recent years, there has been a resurgence of interest in classic cocktails, with many bars and restaurants offering a wide range of classic cocktails on their menus. Some bartenders have even gone so far as to create entire menus dedicated to classic cocktails, offering a modern take on these beloved drinks.

ESSENTIAL INGREDIENTS & TECHNIQUES

Classic cocktails are typically made with a few essential ingredients, including spirits, mixers, and garnishes. These ingredients are the building blocks of classic cocktails, and their quality and balance are essential for a great drink.

- **Spirits:** Classic cocktails are typically made with high-quality spirits, including whiskey, gin, vodka, tequila, and rum. The choice of spirit will depend on the cocktail you are making, and the quality of the spirit will affect the overall flavor and balance of the drink.

- **Mixers:** Mixers are used to add flavor, texture, and balance to a cocktail. Classic cocktails typically use simple mixers such as citrus juice, soda water, and tonic water. Other mixers, such as bitters, vermouth, and liqueurs, can also be used to add complexity and depth to a cocktail.

- **Garnishes:** Garnishes are used to add visual interest and flavor to a cocktail. Classic cocktails typically use simple garnishes such as citrus peels, cherries, and olives. Fresh herbs, spices, and even edible flowers can also be used to create a visually stunning and flavorful drink.

Classic cocktails require a few essential techniques that are used to create a balanced and flavorful drink. These techniques include shaking, stirring, and muddling.

- **Shaking:** Shaking is used to combine ingredients and create a consistent texture and flavor profile. This technique is typically used for cocktails that contain citrus juice or other mixers that need to be fully incorporated.

- **Stirring:** Stirring is used to create a smooth and balanced drink. This technique is typically used for cocktails that contain only spirits and require a gentle mixing to maintain the integrity of the flavors.

- **Muddling**: Muddling is used to extract the flavors and oils from fresh ingredients such as herbs and fruits. This technique is typically used for cocktails that require fresh ingredients and a more complex flavor profile.

TIPS FOR CREATING PERFECT CLASSIC COCKTAILS

Creating the perfect classic cocktail requires skill, precision, and attention to detail. In this chapter, we'll provide step-by-step guidance and practical examples for creating perfect classic cocktails. We'll cover everything from choosing the right ingredients to using the correct techniques to ensure that your cocktail is perfectly balanced and delicious.

Tip 1: Choose High-Quality Ingredients

Choosing high-quality ingredients is essential for creating a great cocktail. Use high-quality spirits, fresh mixers, and seasonal fruits and herbs. The quality of your ingredients will affect the overall flavor and balance of your cocktail.

Tip 2: Measure Your Ingredients

Precision is key when making classic cocktails. Measure your ingredients carefully, using a jigger or a measuring cup, to ensure that your cocktail is perfectly balanced.

Tip 3: Use the Right Glassware

Using the right glassware is important for creating a visually appealing cocktail. Choose the appropriate glass for your cocktail, such as a martini glass for a Martini or a highball glass for a Gin and Tonic.

Tip 4: Ice Matters

The ice you use can affect the texture and temperature of your cocktail. Use large ice cubes or spheres for stirred cocktails, and crushed ice for shaken cocktails.

Tip 5: Shake or Stir with Purpose

Shaking and stirring are two essential techniques for creating classic cocktails. Shaking is used for cocktails that contain citrus juice or other mixers that need to be fully incorporated, while stirring is used for cocktails that contain only spirits. Shake or stir with purpose and confidence to ensure that your cocktail is perfectly mixed.

Tip 6: Garnish with Care

Garnishes are used to add visual interest and flavor to your cocktail. Choose a garnish that complements the flavors of your cocktail and add it with care, ensuring that it doesn't overwhelm the drink.

Example: The Perfect Martini

Ingredients:

- 2 oz gin
- 1 oz dry vermouth
- 1 dash orange bitters
- Lemon twist or olive, for garnish

Instructions:

1. Fill a mixing glass with ice.
2. Add the gin, dry vermouth, and orange bitters.

3. Stir for 20-30 seconds until well-chilled.

4. Strain the mixture into a chilled martini glass.

5. Garnish with a lemon twist or olive.

In conclusion, creating the perfect classic cocktail requires attention to detail, precision, and skill. Choosing high-quality ingredients, measuring carefully, using the right glassware, and shaking or stirring with purpose are all essential for creating a perfectly balanced and delicious cocktail. Remember to garnish with care and creativity, and experiment with new flavors and ingredients to create your own unique twist on classic cocktails.

Modern Cocktails

While classic cocktails have stood the test of time, modern cocktails have emerged as a new and exciting trend in mixology. With an emphasis on fresh and seasonal ingredients, innovative techniques, and unique flavors, modern cocktails offer a fresh take on traditional mixology. In this chapter, we'll explore some of the most popular modern cocktails, their unique ingredients and techniques, and provide tips for creating your own modern cocktails at home. Get ready to discover the newest and most creative cocktails that are taking the mixology world by storm.

IMPORTANCE OF EXPERIMENTATION

Mixology is an art that has been evolving for centuries. From the classic cocktails of the 19th century to the modern twists of today, mixologists have always been pushing the boundaries of what is possible. The key to creating new and innovative drinks is innovation and creativity.

These are the driving forces behind the mixology industry. They inspire bartenders and mixologists to think outside the box and come up with new and exciting drinks that leave a lasting impression on customers and guests. Without innovation and creativity, mixology would become stagnant and lose its appeal. Innovation and creativity are important because they allow mixologists to break the rules and experiment with unconventional ingredients and techniques. They give mixologists the freedom to take risks and try new things that can lead to breakthroughs and help them create drinks that are truly unique and memorable.

To be truly innovative, you must be willing to step outside of your comfort zone. You must be willing to try new things, experiment with new ingredients and techniques, and think outside the box. This can be scary at first, but it is the only way to truly push the boundaries of what is possible. Finding inspiration is also key to unleashing your creative potential and coming up with new and innovative drinks. Inspiration can come from anywhere, whether it's from a new ingredient, a flavor combination that you've never tried before, or a personal experience that inspires you to create something special. It's important to always keep an open mind and be receptive to new ideas and inspirations.

By experimenting with new techniques and ingredients, you can expand your knowledge and expertise, and develop a unique style that sets you apart from other mixologists. In conclusion, Innovation and creativity are what make mixology an art form. They are what allow mixologists to create drinks that are not only delicious but also visually stunning and emotionally engaging. They are what keep customers and guests coming back for more.

MODERN TWISTS ON CLASSIC COCKTAILS

Modern twists on classic cocktails have become a staple in the world of mixology, offering new and innovative ways to enjoy traditional drinks. As a bartender or aspiring mixologist, it's essential to understand the fundamentals of classic cocktails and how to create modern variations that are both unique and delicious. In this chapter, we'll explore the principles behind modern twists on classic cocktails, providing theoretical and information-rich insights to help you create your own modern cocktails.

To create modern twists on classic cocktails, you must first understand the principles behind these drinks. Classic cocktails are typically made with simple ingredients, such as spirits, mixers, and garnishes, that are combined in precise proportions to create a balanced and flavorful drink. Modern twists on classic cocktails involve adding new and innovative ingredients or techniques to create a fresh take on these timeless drinks.

- **Innovative Ingredients:** One way to add a modern twist to a classic cocktail is to incorporate new and innovative ingredients. For example, you might use fresh herbs, fruits, or vegetables to add a unique flavor profile to a traditional cocktail. Other innovative ingredients might include specialty syrups, bitters, or liqueurs that are designed to complement the flavors of the original cocktail.
- **Innovative Techniques:** Another way to add a modern twist to a classic cocktail is to use innovative techniques. For example, you might use molecular gastronomy techniques to create unique textures or infusions. You might also use smoking or infusing techniques to add new flavors or aromas to a traditional cocktail.

MODERN TWISTS EXAMPLES

Let's explore some modern twists on classic cocktails, providing theoretical and information-rich insights to help you create your own modern cocktails.

The Lavender Gin Sour

The Gin Sour is a classic cocktail made with gin, lemon juice, and simple syrup. To give it a modern twist, try adding lavender syrup for a floral and fragrant flavor. Here's how to make a Lavender Gin Sour:

Ingredients:

- 2 oz gin

- 1 oz lemon juice
- 1 oz lavender syrup
- Egg white (optional)
- Lavender sprig, for garnish

Instructions:

1. Fill a shaker with ice.
2. Add gin, lemon juice, and lavender syrup.
3. If using, add egg white.
4. Shake vigorously for 20-30 seconds.
5. Strain into a glass filled with ice.
6. Garnish with a lavender sprig.

The Jalapeño Margarita

The Margarita is a classic cocktail made with tequila, lime juice, and simple syrup. To give it a modern twist, try adding some spice with jalapeño slices or a dash of hot sauce. Here's how to make a Jalapeño Margarita:

Ingredients:

- 2 oz tequila
- 1 oz lime juice
- 1 oz simple syrup
- 2-3 slices of jalapeño
- Salt or chili powder, for rimming (optional)

Instructions:

1. Rim a glass with salt or chili powder (optional).

2. Muddle jalapeño slices in the bottom of a shaker.

3. Add tequila, lime juice, and simple syrup.

4. Add ice and shake vigorously.

5. Strain into the prepared glass and garnish with a jalapeño slice.ù

Modern twists on classic cocktails have become an essential part of mixology, offering new and innovative ways to enjoy traditional drinks. As a bartender or aspiring mixologist, it's important to understand the principles behind these drinks, including the use of innovative ingredients and techniques. By experimenting with new flavors and techniques, you can create your own modernand unique takes on ever-green cocktails. Remember to always balance the flavors of your ingredients, measure carefully, and use the appropriate glassware and garnishes to create a visually appealing and flavorful drink.

CREATION OF NEW AND INNOVATIVE DRINKS

As a bartender or aspiring mixologist, you may be interested in creating new and innovative drinks that stand out from the crowd. Modern twists on the creation of new and innovative drinks can help you do just that. In this chapter, we'll explore the principles behind creating new and innovative drinks, providing theoretical and information-rich insights to help you create your own signature cocktails. Creating new and innovative drinks involves a deep understanding of the principles behind classic cocktails and the ability to think creatively and experiment with new ingredients and techniques. Here are some principles to keep in mind:

Balance is Key: Balance is key when creating new and innovative drinks. You must balance the flavors of your ingredients to create a harmonious and flavorful drink. This includes balancing the sweetness, acidity, and bitterness of your ingredients.

Experiment with New Ingredients: To create new and innovative drinks, you must be willing to experiment with new ingredients. This might include using fresh fruits, herbs, or spices, or incorporating unique liqueurs or spirits. Be sure to taste-test as you go to ensure that the flavors work well together.

Get Creative with Techniques: In addition to experimenting with new ingredients, you can get creative with techniques to create new and innovative drinks. This might include using molecular gastronomy techniques to create unique textures or infusions, or using smoking or infusing techniques to add new flavors or aromas.

MODERN TWISTS ON THE CREATION OF INNOVATIVE DRINKS EXAMPLES

Let's explore some modern twists on the creation of new and innovative drinks, providing theoretical and information-rich insights to help you create your own signature cocktails.

The Grapefruit and Sage Spritz

The Grapefruit and Sage Spritz is a refreshing and flavorful drink that combines grapefruit juice, sage, and Prosecco. Here's how to make it:

Ingredients:

- 1 oz grapefruit juice
- ½ oz sage simple syrup
- Prosecco
- Sage leaves, for garnish

Instructions:

1. Fill a glass with ice.
2. Add grapefruit juice and sage simple syrup.
3. Top with Prosecco.

4. Garnish with sage leaves.

The Lavender Lemonade

The Lavender Lemonade is a floral and refreshing drink that combines lavender syrup, lemon juice, and vodka. Here's how to make it:

Ingredients:

- 2 oz vodka
- 1 oz lavender syrup
- 1 oz lemon juice
- Club soda
- Lavender sprig, for garnish

Instructions:

1. Fill a shaker with ice.
2. Add vodka, lavender syrup, and lemon juice.
3. Shake vigorously for 20-30 seconds.
4. Strain into a glass filled with ice.
5. Top with club soda.
6. Garnish with a lavender sprig.

In conclusion, modern twists on the creation of new and innovative drinks can help you stand out from the crowd and impress your customers or guests with your creativity and skill. Remember to balance your ingredients, experiment with new flavors and techniques, and use appropriate glassware and garnishes to create a visually appealing and flavorful drink. With practice and experimentation, you can create your own signature cocktails and establish yourself as a master of modern mixology.

HOW TO START CREATING NEW VARIATIONS

It can be daunting to come up with new and unique drinks, but with practice and guidance, it can become second nature. In this chapter, we'll provide practical insights and realistic examples on how to practice inventing new cocktails or variations, with step-by-step guidance for easy reference.

Step 1: Start with a Classic Cocktail

One way to practice inventing new cocktails or variations is to start with a classic cocktail as your base. Choose a classic cocktail that you're familiar with, and experiment with different ingredients, techniques, and garnishes to create a new variation. For example, you could create a twist on a classic margarita by adding fresh fruit puree or swapping out the tequila for a different spirit.

Step 2: Experiment with Flavor Combinations

To create new and unique cocktails, you need to experiment with different flavor combinations. Try combining ingredients that you wouldn't normally think to put together, and taste-test as you go to see how the flavors work together. For example, you could try combining a spicy jalapeno syrup with a sweet fruit puree to create a spicy-sweet flavor profile.

Step 3: Get Creative with Techniques

Technique can also play a big role in inventing new cocktails or variations. Experiment with different techniques, such as muddling, shaking, or stirring, to create different textures and flavors in your drinks. For example, you could try shaking a cocktail with egg whites to create a frothy texture, or using a smoking gun to infuse your drinks with smoky flavors.

Step 4: Consider Seasonality and Trends

Consider the seasonality and current trends when inventing new cocktails or variations. Use seasonal ingredients to create drinks that are fresh and relevant, and take inspiration from current trends in the mixology industry. For example, you could create a fall-inspired cocktail with flavors like pumpkin spice or apple cider, or create a drink inspired by the latest cocktail trends on social media.

Step 5: Keep Detailed Notes

When inventing new cocktails or variations, it's important to keep detailed notes of your experiments. Record the ingredients, proportions, techniques, and garnishes that you use, and make notes on how the drink tasted and how it could be improved. This will help you refine your recipes over time and create drinks that are truly unique and delicious.

Remember to start with a classic cocktail as your base, experiment with different flavor combinations and techniques, consider seasonality and trends, and keep detailed notes of your experiments. By following these steps and practicing regularly, you can become a master at inventing new and innovative cocktails that leave a lasting impression on customers and guests.

Advanced Mixology Techniques

If you've been in the mixology game for a while, you may be ready to take your skills to the next level. Advanced mixology techniques can help you elevate your craft and create drinks that are truly unique and memorable. In this chapter, we'll explore some of the most advanced mixology techniques, from barrel aging to molecular mixology, and provide practical insights and guidance to help you master them. Get ready to take your mixology skills to new heights!

MOLECULAR MIXOLOGY TECHNIQUES & TOOLS

Molecular mixology is a cutting-edge approach to mixology that involves using science and technology to create innovative cocktails with unique textures, flavors, and presentations. It's a rapidly growing trend in the mixology industry, and mastering molecular mixology techniques and tools can help you take your craft to the next level. Let's delve into practical insights and realistic examples on molecular mixology techniques and tools.

Techniques:

Spherification: this is a technique that involves creating small spheres or beads of liquid that burst in your mouth, releasing a burst of flavor. To create spherification, you'll need sodium alginate and calcium chloride. Here's how to do it:

- Mix your desired liquid with sodium alginate until it dissolves.
- Using a dropper or syringe, drop the liquid into a solution of calcium chloride.
- The liquid will form into small spheres or beads, which can be strained and rinsed with water before use.

Foam: Foam is a popular molecular mixology technique that involves creating a light, airy foam to top your cocktails. To create foam, you'll need a whipping siphon and a source of gas, such as nitrous oxide. Here's how to do it:

- Combine your desired liquid with a stabilizer, such as lecithin or gelatin.
- Pour the mixture into a whipping siphon and charge it with gas.
- Shake the siphon vigorously to create foam, and dispense it onto your cocktail.

Infusion: Infusion is a technique that involves infusing liquids with different flavors, such as herbs, spices, or fruits. To create an infusion, you'll need a vacuum sealer and a vacuum chamber. Here's how to do it:

- Combine your desired liquid and flavorings in a vacuum-sealable bag.
- Seal the bag using a vacuum sealer, removing as much air as possible.
- Place the bag in a vacuum chamber and apply pressure, which will force the liquid to absorb the flavorings more quickly.

Tools

- **Sous Vide Machine:** A sous vide machine is a device that allows you to cook ingredients at a precise temperature for a specific amount of time. This can be used to infuse flavors, create infused syrups, or even cook ingredients like fruits and vegetables.
- **Rotary Evaporator:** A rotary evaporator is a device that allows you to distill liquids at a low temperature, which can help preserve delicate flavors and aromas. It's often used for creating flavored spirits or creating unique infusions.
- **Liquid Nitrogen:** Liquid nitrogen is often used in molecular mixology to create frozen garnishes or to rapidly freeze ingredients. It's an extremely cold substance, so it must be handled with care and used in a well-ventilated area.

Practical Examples

Cucumber and Lime Spherification

1. To create a unique and flavorful spherification, try combining cucumber juice with lime juice. Here's how to do it:

2. Mix equal parts cucumber juice and lime juice with sodium alginate until it dissolves.

3. Using a dropper or syringe, drop the liquid into a solution of calcium chloride.

4. The liquid will form into small spheres or beads, which can be strained and rinsed with water before use.

Lavender Foam Martini

1. To create a unique and fragrant foam, try infusing gin with lavender using a sous vide machine, then topping it with a lavender foam. Here's how to do it:

2. Infuse gin with fresh lavender using a sous vide machine set to 140 degrees Fahrenheit for 2 hours.

3. Combine the infused gin with a stabilizer, such as lecithin or gelatin, and pour it into a whipping siphon.

4. Charge the siphon with nitrous oxide gas and shake vigorously to create foam.

5. Dispense the foam onto a classic martini, garnished with a sprig of fresh lavender.

Frozen Strawberry Margarita Nitro

1. To create a frozen cocktail with a unique texture, try using liquid nitrogen to freeze fresh strawberries before blending them with tequila and lime juice. Here's how to do it:

2. Freeze fresh strawberries with liquid nitrogen, being sure to handle it with care and use in a well-ventilated area.

3. Blend the frozen strawberries with tequila, lime juice, and ice.

4. Serve in a chilled glass with a lime wedge, for garnish.

CUSTOM SYRUPS, BITTERS & TINCTURES

Creating custom syrups, bitters, and tinctures is a great way to add unique and personalized flavors to your cocktails. By using different herbs, spices, fruits, and other ingredients, you can create flavors that are completely your own. In the following lines, we'll provide practical insights and realistic examples on how to create custom syrups, bitters, and tinctures.

Custom Syrups

Simple Syrup: Simple syrup is a basic syrup made from equal parts sugar and water. To create custom simple syrups, you can add different flavorings, such as herbs, fruits, or spices. Here's how to make it:

- Combine equal parts sugar and water in a saucepan.
- Heat the mixture over medium heat, stirring until the sugar dissolves.
- Add your desired flavorings, such as fresh mint or sliced ginger.
- Simmer the mixture for 10-15 minutes, then remove from heat and let cool.
- Strain out the solids and bottle the syrup for later use.

Fruit Syrup: Fruit syrups are a great way to add fruity flavors to your cocktails. Here's how to make it:

- Combine fresh or frozen fruit with equal parts sugar and water in a saucepan.
- Heat the mixture over medium heat, stirring until the sugar dissolves.
- Simmer the mixture for 10-15 minutes, then remove from heat and let cool.
- Strain out the solids and bottle the syrup for later use.

Custom Bitters

Citrus Bitters: Citrus bitters add a bright and tangy flavor to your cocktails. Here's how to make it:

- Combine dried citrus peels, such as lemon, lime, or orange, with high-proof alcohol, such as vodka or everclear.
- Add additional flavorings, such as herbs or spices, if desired.
- Let the mixture steep for several weeks, shaking the jar periodically.
- Strain out the solids and bottle the bitters for later use.

Spiced Bitters: Spiced bitters add warm and complex flavors to your cocktails. Here's how to make it:

- Combine dried spices, such as cinnamon, cloves, or cardamom, with high-proof alcohol.
- Add additional flavorings, such as herbs or citrus peels, if desired.
- Let the mixture steep for several weeks, shaking the jar periodically.
- Strain out the solids and bottle the bitters for later use.

Custom Tinctures

Herbal Tincture: Herbal tinctures add complex and earthy flavors to your cocktails. Here's how to make it:

- Combine fresh or dried herbs, such as rosemary, thyme, or sage, with high-proof alcohol.
- Let the mixture steep for several weeks, shaking the jar periodically.
- Strain out the solids and bottle the tincture for later use.

Floral Tincture: Floral tinctures add delicate and fragrant flavors to your cocktails. Here's how to make it:

- Combine fresh or dried flowers, such as lavender, rose petals, or elderflower, with high-proof alcohol.
- Let the mixture steep for several weeks, shaking the jar periodically.
- Strain out the solids and bottle the tincture for later use.

Practical Examples

Cinnamon Simple Syrup

- To create a unique and warming simple syrup, try adding cinnamon sticks to your syrup. Here's how to make it:
- Combine equal parts sugar and water in a saucepan.
- Add cinnamon sticks to the mixture and heat over medium heat, stirring until the sugar dissolves.
- Simmer the mixture for 10-15 minutes, then remove from heat and let cool.
- Strain out the cinnamon sticks and bottle the syrup for later use.

Lavender Bitters

- To create a unique and fragrant bitters, try infusing high-proof alcohol with fresh lavender. Here's how to make it:
- Combine dried lavender flowers with high-proof alcohol, such as vodka or everclear.
- Add additional flavorings, such as lemon peel or cinnamon, if desired.
- Let the mixture steep for several weeks, shaking the jar periodically.
- Strain out the solids and bottle the bitters for later use.

Rosemary Tincture

- To create a unique and earthy tincture, try infusing high-proof alcohol with fresh rosemary. Here's how to make it:

- Combine fresh rosemary with high-proof alcohol, such as vodka or everclear.

- Let the mixture steep for several weeks, shaking the jar periodically.

- Strain out the solids and bottle the tincture for later use.

ADVANCED TECHNIQUES FOR IMPRESSIVE DRINKS

Creating unique and impressive drinks requires more than just basic mixology skills. Advanced techniques and tricks can help you create cocktails that are truly memorable and stand out from the crowd. In this chapter, we'll provide practical insights and realistic examples on advanced techniques for creating unique and impressive drinks.

Smoke Infusion: Smoke infusion is a technique that involves infusing your cocktails with the flavor of smoke. This technique can be achieved by using a smoke gun, a handheld device that creates smoke, or by using a smoking box. Here's how to do it:

- Combine your desired ingredients in a shaker with ice.

- Use a smoke gun to infuse the mixture with smoke, or place the mixture in a smoking box and smoke it for several minutes.

- Strain the mixture into a glass and garnish with a smoking herb, such as rosemary or thyme.

Carbonation: Carbonating your cocktails can add a unique and refreshing twist to your drinks. This technique can be achieved by using a soda siphon or a carbonation machine. Here's how to do it:

- Mix your desired ingredients in a shaker with ice.

- Transfer the mixture to a soda siphon or carbonation machine and follow the manufacturer's instructions to carbonate the mixture.

- Serve the carbonated cocktail in a chilled glass with a garnish of your choice.

Fat-Washing: Fat-washing is a technique that involves infusing your cocktails with the flavor of fat, such as bacon or butter. This technique can be achieved by using a blender or by letting the fat sit in the cocktail for a period of time. Here's how to do it:

- Combine your desired fat with your desired alcohol in a blender.
- Blend the mixture until it is well combined and let it sit for several hours.
- Strain the mixture through a fine-mesh strainer to remove any solid pieces of fat.
- Use the infused alcohol to create your desired cocktail.

Flame and Fire: Flame and fire can add an element of drama and excitement to your cocktails. This technique can be achieved by using a torch or by flaming a citrus peel over the cocktail. Here's how to do it:

- Combine your desired ingredients in a shaker with ice.
- Use a torch to light a sprig of fresh herbs, such as rosemary or thyme, on fire.
- Pour the cocktail over the flaming herb and extinguish the flame by covering the glass with a coaster or other object.
- Alternatively, flame a citrus peel over the cocktail by lighting a match, holding the peel over the flame, and squeezing the oils over the cocktail.

Responsible Mixology

As a bartender or mixologist, it's important to not only create delicious and impressive cocktails, but also to prioritize the safety and well-being of your customers. Responsible mixology involves creating and serving drinks in a way that minimizes potential harm and promotes responsible consumption. In the following pages, we'll explore the principles of responsible mixology and provide practical tips for ensuring that you are creating and serving drinks in a responsible manner.

SOCIAL RESPONSIBILITY IN THE DRINKING INDUSTRY

As bartenders and mixologists, it's important to not only focus on creating great drinks, but also to consider the social responsibility of the drinking industry. Serving alcohol comes with the responsibility to ensure that customers are not over-served and that they are safe both inside and outside the establishment.

Responsible Serving Practices: Responsible serving practices involve monitoring customers' alcohol intake and making sure that they are not over-served. Here are some practical examples of responsible serving practices:

- Monitoring the amount of alcohol served to customers
- Cutting off customers who appear to be intoxicated
- Providing non-alcoholic drink options
- Encouraging customers to have a designated driver or using ride-share services

Safety Measures: Safety measures are important for ensuring that customers are safe while on the premises of your establishment. Here are some practical examples of safety measures:

- Training staff to recognize and intervene in potentially dangerous situations
- Providing well-lit areas for customers to park and walk to their vehicles
- Having a plan in place for dealing with customers who have had too much to drink

Maintaining a clean and well-lit establishment

Community Involvement: It's important for establishments to be involved in the local community and to give back in a responsible manner. Here are some practical examples of community involvement:

- Hosting events that benefit local charities or organizations
- Partnering with local businesses to promote community events
- Supporting local law enforcement efforts to prevent drunk driving
- Providing education and training to staff and customers on responsible drinking practices

Environmental Responsibility: It's important for establishments to take steps to minimize their impact on the environment. Here are some practical examples of environmental responsibility:

- Using eco-friendly products, such as biodegradable straws and compostable cups

- Reducing waste by using reusable items, such as glassware and cloth napkins
- Conserving water by using low-flow fixtures and implementing water-saving practices
- Recycling and properly disposing of waste

Practical Examples

The Last Call Program: The Last Call Program is an initiative started by the National Restaurant Association to promote responsible serving practices. The program trains bartenders and servers on how to recognize the signs of intoxication and how to intervene to prevent over-serving. By participating in this program, establishments can demonstrate their commitment to responsible serving practices and provide a safer environment for their customers.

SafeRide Home Program: The SafeRide Home Program is a partnership between local businesses, law enforcement, and ride-share services to provide safe transportation for customers who have had too much to drink. Participating establishments provide vouchers for ride-share services to customers who need a safe ride home. This program not only promotes responsible drinking practices, but also helps to prevent drunk driving and keep the community safe.

Sustainable Sips: Sustainable Sips is a program started by the Green Restaurant Association to promote environmental responsibility in the drinking industry. Participating establishments are required to meet certain sustainability standards, such as using eco-friendly products and implementing waste-reduction practices. By participating in this program, establishments can demonstrate their commitment to environmental responsibility and reduce their impact on the environment.

LOW-ALCOHOL & ALCOHOL-FREE COCKTAILS

As more people are choosing to drink less alcohol or abstain altogether, there is a growing demand for low-alcohol and alcohol-free cocktails. Creating delicious and sophisticated cocktails that are also low in alcohol or completely alcohol-free can be a challenge, but it's an important skill for bartenders and mixologists to master. So, let's explore the principles of creating low-alcohol and alcohol-free cocktails and provide practical examples of how to make delicious and satisfying drinks without the buzz.

Balancing Flavors: Creating low-alcohol and alcohol-free cocktails requires careful attention to flavor balance. Without the kick of alcohol, the flavors need to be bold and complex to make up for the lack of alcohol. Here are some tips for balancing flavors in low-alcohol and alcohol-free cocktails:

- Use fresh ingredients, such as herbs and fruits, to add depth and complexity to the flavor profile.
- Experiment with different bitters and tinctures to add complexity and depth to the flavor profile.
- Consider using alternative sweeteners, such as honey or agave, to add depth and complexity to the flavor profile.

Using Low-Alcohol or Alcohol-Free Base Spirits: Using low-alcohol or alcohol-free base spirits is a key component of creating low-alcohol and alcohol-free cocktails. Here are some examples of low-alcohol or alcohol-free base spirits:

- **Seedlip**: a non-alcoholic distilled spirit made from botanicals
- **Verjus**: a non-alcoholic juice made from unripe grapes
- **Low-alcohol wine or beer:** wines or beers with a lower alcohol content

Garnishing and Presentation: Garnishing and presentation can make a big difference in the appeal of low-alcohol and alcohol-free cocktails. Here are some tips for garnishing and presenting low-alcohol and alcohol-free cocktails:

- Use fresh herbs or edible flowers as a garnish to add color and depth to the presentation.
- Consider serving low-alcohol and alcohol-free cocktails in unique glassware or using unique ice shapes to add interest to the presentation.
- Add a pop of color to the presentation with a brightly colored straw or napkin.

Practical Examples

Seedlip and Tonic

Seedlip and tonic is a simple and refreshing alcohol-free cocktail. Here's how to make it:

- Combine Seedlip, tonic water, and ice in a highball glass.
- Garnish with a slice of cucumber or a sprig of mint.

Low-Alcohol Spritz

A low-alcohol spritz is a refreshing and sophisticated cocktail that is perfect for warm weather. Here's how to make it:

- Combine low-alcohol wine or beer, soda water, and ice in a wine glass.
- Add a splash of Aperol or Campari for color and flavor.
- Garnish with a slice of orange or grapefruit.

Pineapple Ginger Mocktail

This alcohol-free mocktail is a tropical and flavorful drink that is perfect for summer. Here's how to make it:

- Muddle fresh ginger in the bottom of a shaker.
- Add pineapple juice, lime juice, and simple syrup to the shaker.
- Shake the mixture with ice and strain it into a glass filled with ice.
- Garnish with a slice of pineapple or a piece of crystallized ginger.

IMPORTANCE OF RESPONSIBLE SERVICE AND CONSUMPTION

As a bartender or mixologist, you have a responsibility to ensure that your customers are consuming alcohol in a safe and responsible manner. This not only means monitoring their alcohol intake and making sure they do not become over-intoxicated, but also encouraging responsible consumption practices.

The Risks of Over-Consumption: Over-consumption of alcohol can lead to a range of health and safety risks, both for the individual and those around them. These risks include:

- Alcohol poisoning
- Impaired judgment and decision-making
- Increased risk of accidents and injuries
- Increased risk of violence and aggression
- Long-term health problems, such as liver damage and cancer

Promoting Responsible Service: Promoting responsible service means taking steps to ensure that customers are not over-served and that they are consuming alcohol in a safe and responsible manner. Here are some ways to promote responsible service:

- Monitoring customers' alcohol intake and intervening if necessary
- Providing non-alcoholic drink options
- Encouraging customers to have a designated driver or using ride-share services
- Providing food options to help absorb alcohol
- Training staff or colleagues on responsible serving practices

Encouraging Responsible Consumption: Encouraging responsible consumption means educating customers on the risks of over-consumption and promoting responsible drinking practices. Here are some ways to encourage responsible consumption:

- Educating customers on the risks of over-consumption
- Promoting moderation and responsible drinking practices

- Encouraging customers to drink water between alcoholic drinks
- Encouraging customers to eat food while drinking

Legal and Ethical Obligations: In addition to the moral responsibility of promoting responsible service and consumption, there are also legal and ethical obligations. These obligations include:

- Compliance with laws and regulations related to alcohol service and consumption
- Ethical considerations related to promoting responsible drinking practices and avoiding marketing to minors or vulnerable populations

CONCLUSION

Mixology is a craft that is constantly evolving and expanding. As a mixologist, you have the opportunity to create unique and memorable experiences for your customers, and the possibilities are endless. Throughout this book, we've explored the various aspects of mixology, including the basic building blocks, mixing techniques, classic cocktails, modern twists, advanced techniques, and responsible service and consumption.

By mastering these techniques, you can create drinks that not only taste great but also look and smell amazing. You can use your creativity and imagination to come up with new and innovative drinks that will surprise and delight your customers. The art of mixology is not just about making drinks but about creating an experience that your customers will remember long after they leave your establishment.

In the beginning, we explored the basic building blocks of mixology, including ingredients and tools, and the principles of dilution, ice, and temperature. These foundational elements provide a solid base upon which to build your mixology skills. We then moved on to mixing techniques, including stirring, shaking, and layering. These techniques are essential for creating perfectly balanced cocktails that look and taste amazing. We also explored the art of presentation, including garnishing, layering, rimming, and using edible flowers.

The history and evolution of classic cocktails provide a wealth of inspiration for modern twists and variations. We explored the essential ingredients and techniques for classic cocktails, providing practical tips for creating perfect drinks every time. We also examined the principles of creativity and innovation, providing guidance on how to invent new cocktails and variations.

In the advanced techniques chapter, we explored the world of molecular mixology and the tools and techniques used to create unique and impressive drinks. We also explored the creation of custom syrups, bitters, and tinctures, providing practical guidance for aspiring mixologists.

Finally, we examined the importance of responsible service and consumption. As mixologists, we have a responsibility to ensure that our customers are consuming alcohol in a safe and responsible manner. We explored the risks of over-consumption and provided practical examples of how to promote responsible alcohol consumption.

In conclusion, the art of mixology is a constantly evolving craft that requires creativity, skill, and dedication. By mastering the techniques and principles explored in this book, you can create unique and memorable experiences for your customers. Remember to never stop learning, experimenting, and pushing the boundaries of what's possible. With passion, creativity, and a commitment to responsible service and consumption, you can create drinks that will delight and inspire your customers for years to come. Cheers to the art of mixology!

BOOK 2
CLASSIC COCKTAILS

INTRODUCTION

Welcome to the world of classic cocktails! For centuries, cocktails have been a staple of social gatherings, and they continue to captivate us today. From the timeless Old Fashioned to the elegant Martini, classic cocktails have stood the test of time and are beloved by generations of drinkers. In this book, we will take a deep dive into the world of classic cocktails, exploring the history and evolution of these iconic drinks, as well as the techniques and ingredients that make them so special. Whether you're a seasoned mixologist or a cocktail enthusiast just starting out, this book will provide you with everything you need to know to create delicious, perfectly balanced classic cocktails.

We'll begin by exploring the origins of classic cocktails, tracing their history back to the early days of mixology and the speakeasy era. Along the way, we'll uncover fascinating stories and little-known facts about some of the world's most famous cocktails, from the Manhattan to the Daiquiri. Next, we'll dive into the art and science of cocktail making, examining the essential tools and techniques that every aspiring bartender needs to know. From shaking and stirring to muddling and straining, we'll cover it all, giving you the skills and confidence you need to create perfect cocktails every time.

Finally, we'll explore some of the lesser-known classic cocktails, introducing you to hidden gems that are sure to become new favorites. With recipes and tips for everything from the Sazerac to the Singapore Sling, you'll have everything you need to impress your friends and family with your cocktail-making skills. So whether you're looking to expand your knowledge of classic cocktails, or simply want to enjoy a delicious drink at home, this book is the perfect companion. So sit back, relax, and let's explore the world of classic cocktails together.

Some Theory

Classic cocktails have been a mainstay of mixology for over a century, but what is it about these drinks that have stood the test of time? To truly appreciate the beauty of a classic cocktail, it's essential to understand its rich history and the cultural context that brought it to life. In this introductory chapter, we'll explore the fascinating history of classic cocktails and why they continue to be popular today. From their origins in speakeasies to their role in Hollywood glamour, classic cocktails have a story to tell.

HISTORY OF CLASSIC COCKTAILS

The history of classic cocktails is a vast and fascinating subject, one that encompasses centuries of social and cultural change, as well as the evolution of drinking and bartending practices. From the early days of mixology to the modern era of craft cocktails, the story of classic cocktails is a multifaceted one that offers insights into the development of drinking culture, social mores, and the art of mixology itself.

In the early days of cocktails, around the late 18th and early 19th centuries, the drinks were simple, consisting of just a few ingredients like spirits, bitters, and sugar. These early cocktails, such as the Sazerac, the Gin Sour, and the Mint Julep, were often prescribed as medicinal remedies and were served in small portions.

As cocktails grew in popularity, they became more complex and varied, with bartenders experimenting with different spirits, mixers, and garnishes. During the 19th century, many classic cocktails were born, including the Old Fashioned, Manhattan, and Martini. These drinks are still enjoyed today, and are considered some of the most iconic cocktails of all time.

One of the most significant periods in the history of classic cocktails was the Prohibition era of the 1920s. With the production and sale of alcohol outlawed in the United States, speakeasies began to pop up across the country, offering illicit drinks to patrons. Bartenders at these underground establishments became skilled at mixing and serving classic cocktails, and the era is often credited with helping to popularize drinks like the Gin Fizz and the Sidecar.

After the repeal of Prohibition, classic cocktails continued to evolve, with new ingredients and techniques being introduced. The 1950s and 60s saw the rise of tropical cocktails like the Mai Tai and the Zombie, while the 1970s and 80s brought about the popularity of fruity and sweet drinks like the Piña Colada and the Sex on the Beach.

Today, classic cocktails continue to be a staple of social gatherings and bar menus around the world. Many bars and bartenders are rediscovering the art of classic cocktail making, and are putting their own modern twist on timeless drinks. Craft cocktails, which are typically made with high-quality ingredients and complex flavors, have become increasingly popular in recent years, and have helped to further elevate the status of classic cocktails in the world of mixology.

The history of classic cocktails is not only a story of drinks, but also a story of people and culture. Classic cocktails have been the drink of choice for artists, writers, and cultural icons throughout history, from Hemingway to Sinatra, and continue to be associated with sophistication, glamour, and refinement. As the world of cocktails continues to evolve, one thing is certain: classic cocktails will always hold a special place in the hearts of drinkers and mixologists alike.

WHAT MAKES A COCKTAIL CLASSIC?

The term "classic cocktail" typically refers to a drink that has stood the test of time and is widely recognized as a symbol of cocktail culture. But what is it that makes a cocktail a classic? Is it the ingredients, the preparation method, or something else entirely? In this chapter, we will explore the key characteristics that define a classic cocktail.

First and foremost, a classic cocktail is one that has been around for a long time and has endured through the years. Most classic cocktails were created during the late 19th and early 20th centuries, and have remained popular ever since. These drinks have stood the test of time, and are beloved by generations of drinkers.

Another defining characteristic of a classic cocktail is that it typically consists of a few key ingredients, often including a base spirit, a sweetener, and bitters. Classic cocktails are generally not overly complicated, and rely on simple ingredients and preparation methods to create a balanced and flavorful drink.

In addition to the ingredients, the preparation method is also an important part of what makes a cocktail classic. Classic cocktails are typically prepared in a specific way, often involving techniques like stirring, shaking, or muddling. These techniques are used to blend the ingredients and create a consistent flavor profile. The presentation of a classic cocktail is also an important part of what makes it a classic. Classic cocktails are often served in elegant glassware, and are garnished with simple yet effective garnishes, such as a lemon twist or a cherry. The overall presentation of a classic cocktail is meant to be visually appealing and to enhance the drinking experience.

Finally, a classic cocktail has a story and a history behind it. Many classic cocktails have a fascinating backstory, often involving famous bartenders or historical events. The history and tradition behind a classic cocktail is part of what makes it so special and enduring. In conclusion, a classic cocktail is defined by its longevity, simplicity, preparation method, presentation, and history. These characteristics combine to create a drink that is timeless and enduring, and that continues to captivate and delight drinkers around the world. Whether you're a seasoned mixologist or a cocktail enthusiast just starting out, classic cocktails offer a rich and rewarding world to explore.

WHY CLASSIC COCKTAILS ARE STILL POPULAR

Despite the proliferation of new and innovative cocktails in recent years, classic cocktails remain as popular as ever. What is it about these timeless drinks that continues to captivate and inspire drinkers around the world? In this chapter, we will explore the many reasons why classic cocktails have stood the test of time and remain a beloved part of cocktail culture. One of the primary reasons for the enduring popularity of classic cocktails is their simplicity. Classic cocktails typically consist of just a few high-quality ingredients, such as a base spirit, a sweetener, and bitters. This simplicity not only makes classic cocktails easy to prepare, but it also allows the flavors of the ingredients to shine through, resulting in a balanced and harmonious drink.

Another reason for the popularity of classic cocktails is their versatility. Many classic cocktails can be customized to suit individual tastes, with variations on the ingredients and preparation methods. This versatility allows classic cocktails to be enjoyed in a variety of settings, from a casual night at home to a formal cocktail party. Classic cocktails are also associated with a certain sense of sophistication and glamour. These drinks have a rich history and tradition behind them, and are often associated with famous bartenders, celebrities, and cultural icons. This sense of history and glamour adds to the appeal of classic cocktails, and makes them a popular choice for special occasions and events.

The popularity of classic cocktails can also be attributed to their versatility in terms of serving temperature. Many classic cocktails can be enjoyed hot or cold, and are served in a variety of glassware. This versatility makes classic cocktails suitable for any season or occasion, from a hot toddy on a winter's night to a refreshing gin and tonic on a hot summer day. Finally, the enduring popularity of classic cocktails can be attributed to the fact that they are simply delicious. Classic cocktails have been perfected over many years, with each ingredient and preparation method carefully chosen to create a drink that is both balanced and flavorful. These drinks are a true testament to the art and science of mixology, and continue to delight and inspire drinkers around the world.

In conclusion, the enduring popularity of classic cocktails can be attributed to their simplicity, versatility, history, glamour, and deliciousness. These drinks have stood the test of time and continue to captivate and inspire new generations of cocktail enthusiasts.

THE CLASSICS

OLD FASHIONED

The Old Fashioned is one of the most iconic and beloved classic cocktails. Made with just a few simple ingredients, this drink has stood the test of time and remains a popular choice for cocktail enthusiasts around the world. In this chapter, we will explore the history and evolution of the Old Fashioned, as well as the ingredients and techniques that make this drink so special.

The history of the Old Fashioned dates back to the early days of mixology, and its origins are somewhat shrouded in mystery. Some say the drink was first made in the late 1800s, while others believe it was first created in the early 1900s. Regardless of its exact origins, the Old Fashioned quickly became a popular drink, and has remained a staple of cocktail culture ever since.

The traditional recipe for an Old Fashioned is simple: it consists of a sugar cube, a few dashes of bitters, a splash of water, and a shot of bourbon or rye whiskey. The ingredients are muddled together to create a syrup, and then the drink is finished with a large ice cube and a twist of citrus peel. This simple recipe allows the flavors of the whiskey and the bitters to shine through, resulting in a balanced and harmonious drink.

Over the years, variations on the Old Fashioned have emerged, with bartenders experimenting with different spirits, bitters, and sweeteners. Some variations include the use of fruit, such as muddled cherries or orange slices, or the addition of club soda to create a fizzy version of the drink. Despite these variations, the traditional Old Fashioned remains the most popular and beloved version of the drink.

One of the key elements that sets the Old Fashioned apart from other cocktails is the use of bitters. Bitters are a type of flavored alcohol that are made by infusing botanicals, herbs, and spices in high-proof spirits. The addition of bitters to the Old Fashioned helps to balance the sweetness of the sugar and the richness of the whiskey, resulting in a drink that is complex and flavorful.

Another important element of the Old Fashioned is the use of high-quality ingredients. Because this drink is so simple, each ingredient needs to be of the highest quality to ensure that the drink is as delicious as possible. This means using a high-quality whiskey, fresh citrus peel, and high-quality bitters.

MARTINI

This drink, made with just a few simple ingredients, has been a favorite of cocktail enthusiasts for over a century. In this chapter, we will explore the history and evolution of the Martini, as well as the ingredients and techniques that make this drink so special.

The origins of the Martini are somewhat murky, with many theories about its creation. Some believe that it was first made in the late 1800s, while others believe it was created in the early 1900s. Regardless of its origins, the Martini quickly became a popular drink and has remained a staple of cocktail culture ever since. The traditional recipe for a Martini is simple: it consists of gin and dry vermouth, stirred or shaken together with ice, and garnished with a twist of citrus peel or an olive. The ratios of gin to vermouth can vary, with some drinkers preferring a drier Martini with just a splash of vermouth, while others prefer a more vermouth-forward drink.

One of the key elements that sets the Martini apart from other cocktails is the use of gin. Gin is a spirit made from juniper berries and other botanicals, and its unique flavor profile makes it the perfect base for the Martini. The addition of dry vermouth helps to balance the gin's herbal and floral notes, resulting in a drink that is complex and sophisticated.

Over the years, variations on the Martini have emerged, with bartenders experimenting with different types of gin, vermouth, and garnishes. Some variations include the use of vodka instead of gin, or the addition of fruit juice or other flavorings to create a flavored Martini. Despite these variations, the traditional Martini remains the most popular and beloved version of the drink.

MANHATTAN

The Manhattan is a classic cocktail that has been a favorite of drinkers for over a century. Made with just a few simple ingredients, this drink is beloved for its rich flavor and sophisticated taste. In this chapter, we will explore the history and evolution of the Manhattan, as well as the ingredients and techniques that make this drink so special.

The origins of the Manhattan are somewhat unclear, with several theories about its creation. Some believe that it was first made in the late 1800s, while others believe it was created in the early 1900s. Regardless of its origins, the Manhattan quickly became a popular drink and has remained a staple of cocktail culture ever since.

The traditional recipe for a Manhattan is simple: it consists of rye whiskey, sweet vermouth, and bitters, stirred together with ice and garnished with a cherry. The ratios of whiskey to vermouth can vary, with some drinkers preferring a drier Manhattan with just a splash of vermouth, while others prefer a sweeter drink with a more vermouth-forward flavor.

One of the key elements that sets the Manhattan apart from other cocktails is the use of rye whiskey. Rye whiskey is a type of whiskey made from a mash of at least 51% rye, and its unique flavor profile makes it the perfect base for the Manhattan. The addition of sweet vermouth helps to balance the rye's spicy notes, resulting in a drink that is complex and flavorful.

Over the years, variations on the Manhattan have emerged, with bartenders experimenting with different types of whiskey, vermouth, and garnishes. Some variations include the use of bourbon instead of rye whiskey, or the addition of fruit juice or other flavorings to create a flavored Manhattan. Despite these variations, the traditional Manhattan remains the most popular and beloved version of the drink.

NEGRONI

The Negroni is a classic cocktail that has gained a tremendous following in recent years. Made with just three simple ingredients, this drink is beloved for its bold flavor and unique taste. In this chapter, we will explore the history and evolution of the Negroni, as well as the ingredients and techniques that make this drink so special.

The Negroni is believed to have been created in Italy in the early 1900s, when Count Camillo Negroni asked a bartender to make his Americano cocktail stronger by replacing the soda water with gin. The resulting drink became known as the Negroni, and has remained a beloved drink in Italy ever since.

The traditional recipe for a Negroni is simple: it consists of equal parts gin, sweet vermouth, and Campari, stirred together with ice and garnished with an orange peel. The ratios of each ingredient can be adjusted to suit individual tastes, with some drinkers preferring a stronger gin flavor, while others prefer a more vermouth-forward drink.

One of the key elements that sets the Negroni apart from other cocktails is the use of Campari. Campari is a type of bitter liqueur that is made from a blend of herbs, spices, and fruit. Its unique flavor profile adds a bold and bitter note to the drink, which is balanced by the sweetness of the vermouth and the botanicals of the gin. Over the years, variations on the Negroni have emerged, with bartenders experimenting with different types of gin, vermouth, and bitter liqueurs. Some variations include the use of mezcal instead of gin, or the addition of other bitter liqueurs to create a more complex flavor profile. Despite these variations, the traditional Negroni remains the most popular and beloved version of the drink.

SAZERAC

The Sazerac is a classic cocktail that originated in New Orleans, Louisiana, and is believed to be one of the oldest cocktails in America. Made with just a few simple ingredients, this drink is beloved for its rich flavor and unique taste. In this chapter, we will explore the history and evolution of the Sazerac, as well as the ingredients and techniques that make this drink so special.

The origins of the Sazerac can be traced back to the early 1800s, when it was first made with a combination of brandy, absinthe, bitters, and sugar. Over time, the recipe evolved, with rye whiskey replacing the brandy and Peychaud's Bitters replacing the original bitters. The drink also underwent a name change, from the "Sazerac Cocktail" to simply the "Sazerac."

The traditional recipe for a Sazerac is simple: it consists of rye whiskey, Peychaud's Bitters, a sugar cube, and absinthe, stirred together with ice and garnished with a twist of lemon peel. The use of rye whiskey gives the drink a bold and spicy flavor, while the absinthe adds a subtle herbal note.

One of the key elements that sets the Sazerac apart from other cocktails is the use of absinthe. Absinthe is a type of alcoholic spirit made from a combination of herbs, including wormwood, anise, and fennel. It is typically used as a flavoring agent, rather than a base spirit, and adds a unique and complex flavor to the drink.

DAIQUIRI

Made with just a few simple ingredients, this drink is beloved for its refreshing taste and easy-drinking nature. In this chapter, we will explore the history and evolution of the Daiquiri, as well as the ingredients and techniques that make this drink so special. The origins of the Daiquiri can be traced back to Cuba in the early 1900s, where it was first made with a combination of rum, lime juice, and sugar. Over time, the recipe evolved, with the addition of ice and the use of different types of rum.

The traditional recipe for a Daiquiri is simple: it consists of white rum, lime juice, and simple syrup, shaken together with ice and strained into a chilled glass. The use of white rum gives the drink a light and crisp flavor, while the lime juice adds a tart and refreshing note. One of the key elements that sets the Daiquiri apart from other cocktails is the use of fresh lime juice. Using fresh lime juice instead of pre-made mixers adds a bright and authentic flavor to the drink. Similarly, using high-quality white rum ensures that the drink is as delicious as possible.

Over the years, variations on the Daiquiri have emerged, with bartenders experimenting with different types of rum, juices, and sweeteners. Some variations include the use of dark rum, which adds a richer and more complex flavor to the drink, or the addition of fruit juices like strawberry or pineapple to create a flavored Daiquiri.

MARGARITA

Made with tequila, lime juice, and orange liqueur, this drink is beloved for its refreshing taste and versatility. In this chapter, we will explore the history and evolution of the Margarita, as well as the ingredients and techniques that make this drink so special. The origins of the Margarita are somewhat unclear, with several theories about its creation. Some believe that it was first made in the late 1930s or early 1940s, while others believe it was created in the late 1940s or early 1950s. Regardless of its origins, the Margarita quickly became a popular drink and has remained a staple of cocktail culture ever since.

The traditional recipe for a Margarita is simple: it consists of tequila, lime juice, and orange liqueur, shaken together with ice and served in a salt-rimmed glass. The use of tequila gives the drink a bold and distinctive flavor, while the lime juice adds a tart and refreshing note. The addition of orange liqueur helps to balance the flavors of the tequila and lime juice, resulting in a drink that is both sweet and tart. One of the key elements that sets the Margarita apart from other cocktails is the use of tequila. Tequila is a type of distilled spirit made from the blue agave plant, which is grown in Mexico. Its unique flavor profile makes it the perfect base for the Margarita. The addition of lime juice and orange liqueur helps to balance the tequila's bold and spicy notes, resulting in a drink that is complex and flavorful.

Over the years, variations on the Margarita have emerged, with bartenders experimenting with different types of tequila, lime juice, and orange liqueur. Some variations include the use of different types of tequila, such as reposado or añejo tequila, or the addition of other flavorings, such as fruit purees or chili peppers.

SIDECAR

The Sidecar is a classic cocktail that has been enjoyed by drinkers for over a century. Made with cognac, orange liqueur, and lemon juice, this drink is beloved for its smooth and sophisticated flavor. In this chapter, we will explore the history and evolution of the Sidecar, as well as the ingredients and techniques that make this drink so special. The origins of the Sidecar can be traced back to France in the early 1900s, where it was first made with a combination of cognac, Cointreau, and lemon juice. Over time, the recipe evolved, with the addition of different types of orange liqueur and variations on the ratios of the ingredients.

The traditional recipe for a Sidecar is simple: it consists of cognac, orange liqueur, and lemon juice, shaken together with ice and served in a sugar-rimmed glass. The use of cognac gives the drink a rich and complex flavor, while the orange liqueur adds a sweet and floral note. The addition of lemon juice helps to balance the sweetness of the orange liqueur and gives the drink a tart and refreshing finish. One of the key elements that sets the Sidecar apart from other cocktails is the use of cognac. Cognac is a type of brandy that is made in the Cognac region of France, and is known for its rich and complex flavor. Its use in the Sidecar gives the drink a sophisticated and elegant taste that is perfect for special occasions.

Over the years, variations on the Sidecar have emerged, with bartenders experimenting with different types of cognac, orange liqueur, and lemon juice. Some variations include the use of different types of orange liqueur, such as Grand Marnier or triple sec, or the addition of other flavorings, such as ginger or honey syrup.

GIN & TONIC

The Gin & Tonic is a classic cocktail that has been enjoyed by drinkers for over a century. Made with gin and tonic water, this drink is beloved for its refreshing taste and versatility. In this chapter, we will explore the history and evolution of the Gin & Tonic, as well as the ingredients and techniques that make this drink so special.

The origins of the Gin & Tonic can be traced back to the British East India Company in the 19th century. British soldiers stationed in India were known to add quinine, a medication used to treat malaria, to their tonic water in order to make it more palatable. This led to the creation of the Gin & Tonic, which combined gin, tonic water, and lime juice to create a refreshing and medicinal drink.

The traditional recipe for a Gin & Tonic is simple: it consists of gin, tonic water, and lime juice, served in a tall glass over ice. The use of gin gives the drink a bold and herbal flavor, while the tonic water adds a slightly bitter note and a carbonated fizz. The addition of lime juice helps to balance the flavors of the gin and tonic water, resulting in a drink that is both tart and refreshing.

One of the key elements that sets the Gin & Tonic apart from other cocktails is the use of tonic water. Tonic water is a carbonated soft drink that is flavored with quinine, a bitter compound found in the bark of the cinchona tree. The addition of tonic water to gin creates a unique and complex flavor profile that is both bitter and refreshing.

Over the years, variations on the Gin & Tonic have emerged, with bartenders experimenting with different types of gin, tonic water, and garnishes. Some variations include the use of different types of gin, such as London Dry gin or Old Tom gin, or the addition of other flavorings, such as cucumber or mint.

WHISKEY SOUR

The Whiskey Sour is a classic cocktail that has been enjoyed by drinkers for over a century. Made with whiskey, lemon juice, and simple syrup, this drink is beloved for its sweet and sour flavor and smooth texture. In this chapter, we will explore the history and evolution of the Whiskey Sour, as well as the ingredients and techniques that make this drink so special.

The origins of the Whiskey Sour can be traced back to the 1860s, where it was first made with a combination of whiskey, lemon juice, sugar, and ice. Over time, the recipe evolved, with the addition of different types of whiskey and variations on the ratios of the ingredients. The traditional recipe for a Whiskey Sour is simple: it consists of whiskey, lemon juice, and simple syrup, shaken together with ice and served in a chilled glass. The use of whiskey gives the drink a rich and complex flavor, while the lemon juice adds a tart and refreshing note. The addition of simple syrup helps to balance the flavors of the whiskey and lemon juice, resulting in a drink that is both sweet and sour.

One of the key elements that sets the Whiskey Sour apart from other cocktails is the use of whiskey. Whiskey is a type of distilled spirit made from grain, which can include barley, corn, rye, or wheat. Its unique flavor profile makes it the perfect base for the Whiskey Sour. The addition of lemon juice and simple syrup helps to balance the whiskey's bold and smoky notes, resulting in a drink that is both complex and flavorful.

Over the years, variations on the Whiskey Sour have emerged, with bartenders experimenting with different types of whiskey, lemon juice, and sweeteners. Some variations include the use of different types of whiskey, such as bourbon or rye whiskey, or the addition of other flavorings, such as egg white or bitters.

WHISKEY SOUR

Made with whiskey, lemon juice, and simple syrup, this drink is beloved for its sweet and sour flavor and smooth texture. In this chapter, we will explore the history and evolution of the Whiskey Sour, as well as the ingredients and techniques that make this drink so special. The origins of the Whiskey Sour can be traced back to the 1860s, where it was first made with a combination of whiskey, lemon juice, sugar, and ice. Over time, the recipe evolved, with the addition of different types of whiskey and variations on the ratios of the ingredients.

The traditional recipe for a Whiskey Sour is simple: it consists of whiskey, lemon juice, and simple syrup, shaken together with ice and served in a chilled glass. The use of whiskey gives the drink a rich and complex flavor, while the lemon juice adds a tart and refreshing note. The addition of simple syrup helps to balance the flavors of the whiskey and lemon juice, resulting in a drink that is both sweet and sour.

One of the key elements that sets the Whiskey Sour apart from other cocktails is the use of whiskey. Whiskey is a type of distilled spirit made from grain, which can include barley, corn, rye, or wheat. Its unique flavor profile makes it the perfect base for the Whiskey Sour. The addition of lemon juice and simple syrup helps to balance the whiskey's bold and smoky notes, resulting in a drink that is both complex and flavorful.

Over the years, variations on the Whiskey Sour have emerged, with bartenders experimenting with different types of whiskey, lemon juice, and sweeteners. Some variations include the use of different types of whiskey, such as bourbon or rye whiskey, or the addition of other flavorings, such as egg white or bitters.

The Evolution of Classic Cocktails

Classic cocktails have stood the test of time, but that doesn't mean they haven't evolved over the years. In fact, the evolution of classic cocktails has been a key part of their continued popularity. In this chapter, we'll explore how modern mixologists have put their own spin on classic recipes, using unique ingredients and techniques to create new variations on old favorites. We'll also take a look at what the future holds for classic cocktails, and how they will continue to evolve and adapt to changing tastes and trends. So, get ready to discover the exciting new world of classic cocktails, and the creative twists that are keeping them fresh and relevant.

MODERN TWISTS ON CLASSIC RECIPES

Modern twists on classic cocktail recipes have indeed become increasingly popular in the world of cocktails. With the rise of the craft cocktail movement, bartenders and mixologists are constantly innovating and experimenting with new flavors, ingredients, and techniques. In this chapter, we will explore some of the most popular modern twists on classic cocktail recipes, as well as the ingredients and techniques that make them so special.

One popular modern twist on a classic recipe is the Espresso Martini. This drink, which is made with vodka, freshly brewed espresso, and coffee liqueur, has become a staple in many modern bars and restaurants. The addition of espresso adds a rich and bold flavor to the drink, while the coffee liqueur provides a subtle sweetness that balances out the bitterness of the espresso. Some bartenders may also add a touch of simple syrup or a garnish of espresso beans to enhance the flavor and presentation of the drink.

Another popular modern twist is the Mezcal Margarita. This drink, which is made with mezcal, lime juice, and agave syrup, offers a smoky and complex flavor profile that is a departure from the classic Margarita. Mezcal is a type of distilled spirit made from the agave plant, and is known for its bold and smoky flavor. The addition of agave syrup and lime juice helps to balance out the smokiness of the mezcal, resulting in a drink that is both refreshing and flavorful.

A third modern twist on a classic cocktail is the Elderflower Gimlet. This drink, which is made with gin, lime juice, and elderflower liqueur, offers a floral and delicate flavor profile that is a departure from the traditional Gimlet. Elderflower liqueur is made from the flowers of the elderberry plant, and adds a subtle sweetness and floral note to the drink. The addition of lime juice helps to balance out the sweetness of the elderflower liqueur, resulting in a drink that is both refreshing and complex.

Another popular modern twist is the Spicy Margarita. This drink, which is made with tequila, lime juice, and jalapeno syrup, offers a spicy and bold flavor profile that is a departure from the classic Margarita. The addition of jalapeno syrup provides a subtle heat that balances out the tartness of the lime juice, resulting in a drink that is both refreshing and spicy.

Finally, the Old Fashioned has also received a modern twist with the addition of flavored bitters. While the traditional Old Fashioned is made with whiskey, sugar, bitters, and a citrus twist, modern variations may include flavored bitters, such as chocolate or lavender, for added complexity and depth of flavor.

In conclusion, modern twists on classic cocktail recipes have become a popular trend in the world of mixology, as bartenders and mixologists continue to push the boundaries of what is possible with cocktails. By experimenting with new ingredients and techniques, they are able to create drinks that are both familiar and innovative, offering a new perspective on classic recipes. Exploring modern twists on classic cocktail recipes offers a rich and rewarding world to explore for both seasoned mixologists and cocktail enthusiasts.

USING UNIQUE INGREDIENTS AND TECHNIQUES

Using unique ingredients and techniques in cocktail-making is a way for bartenders and mixologists to differentiate themselves and stand out in the crowded bar scene. One example of a unique ingredient that has gained popularity in recent years is matcha powder. Matcha is a type of green tea that has been ground into a fine powder, and is known for its earthy and slightly bitter flavor. Bartenders and mixologists have been using matcha powder to add a unique twist to classic cocktails, such as the Gin and Tonic or the Margarita. By adding a small amount of matcha powder to the cocktail, they are able to create a vibrant green color and a subtle earthy flavor that enhances the overall experience of the drink.

Another unique ingredient that has gained popularity is aquafaba, which is the liquid from a can of chickpeas. Aquafaba is a vegan alternative to egg whites, and can be used to create a foamy texture in cocktails. This technique is particularly useful in creating vegan versions of classic cocktails such as the Whiskey Sour or the Clover Club. By using aquafaba instead of egg whites, bartenders and mixologists are able to create a similar texture and mouthfeel without using animal products.

A third unique ingredient that has been used in cocktails is activated charcoal. Activated charcoal is a type of charcoal that has been treated with oxygen to create a porous surface, which makes it an effective filter for removing impurities. Bartenders and mixologists have been using activated charcoal to create dramatic black cocktails, such as the Black Manhattan or the Black Daiquiri. By adding a small amount of activated charcoal to the cocktail, they are able to create a unique and striking visual effect that enhances the overall experience of the drink.

In addition to unique ingredients, bartenders and mixologists are also experimenting with unique techniques to create new and exciting cocktails. One example is the use of molecular gastronomy techniques, such as foams, gels, and spherification. These techniques involve using chemicals such as agar agar or sodium alginate to create textures and shapes that are not possible with traditional ingredients. For example, a bartender may use spherification to create a small sphere of a cocktail ingredient, such as a lime juice, which can then be added to the cocktail for a unique burst of flavor.

Another unique technique that has gained popularity is smoking cocktails. This technique involves using a smoking gun or other device to infuse a cocktail with smoke, which can add a unique and complex flavor profile. For example, a bartender may smoke a Whiskey Sour by adding wood chips to a smoking gun and infusing the smoke into the cocktail shaker before shaking the drink. The resulting cocktail will have a subtle smoky flavor that enhances the whiskey and balances out the tartness of the lemon juice.

By experimenting with ingredients such as matcha powder, aquafaba, and activated charcoal, they are able to add new flavor profiles and visual elements to classic cocktails. Additionally, using techniques such as molecular gastronomy and smoking cocktails can create unique textures and flavor profiles that are not possible with traditional ingredients. By incorporating these unique ingredients and techniques, bartenders and mixologists are able to create a truly memorable drinking experience for their customers.

THE FUTURE OF CLASSIC COCKTAILS

The future of classic cocktails is an exciting and rapidly evolving landscape. With the rise of the craft cocktail movement and the increasing popularity of unique ingredients and techniques, there is a lot to look forward to in the world of mixology. In this chapter, we will explore some of the trends and innovations that are shaping the future of classic cocktails, as well as some real-life examples of how bartenders and mixologists are pushing the boundaries of what is possible.

One trend that is emerging in the world of classic cocktails is the use of sustainable and locally sourced ingredients. With a growing focus on sustainability and reducing carbon footprints, bartenders and mixologists are turning to locally sourced and seasonal ingredients to create their cocktails. For example, a bartender in San Francisco might use locally grown Meyer lemons in their Whiskey Sour, while a bartender in New York might use locally harvested honey in their Old Fashioned. By using ingredients that are grown and harvested in their local communities, bartenders and mixologists are able to create cocktails that are not only delicious, but also have a smaller environmental impact.

Another trend in the future of classic cocktails is the use of technology. As technology continues to advance, bartenders and mixologists are finding new ways to incorporate it into their cocktail-making process. For example, some bars are using machines that can automatically chill and dispense cocktails, reducing wait times and increasing efficiency. Others are experimenting with augmented reality or virtual reality experiences that allow customers to interact with the cocktail-making process in new and innovative ways.

In addition to sustainability and technology, there is also a growing interest in the health and wellness benefits of cocktails. With the rise of the wellness movement and the increasing popularity of low-alcohol or non-alcoholic drinks, bartenders and mixologists are finding new ways to create cocktails that are both delicious and health-conscious. For example, a bartender might use fresh fruits and vegetables in their cocktails to add vitamins and nutrients, or incorporate herbal infusions that have been traditionally used for medicinal purposes.

One real-life example of the future of classic cocktails is the use of fermentation. Fermentation is a process that has been used for centuries in the production of beer and wine, but is now being used in cocktail-making as well. Fermented ingredients can add unique and complex flavors to cocktails, as well as providing health benefits such as probiotics. For example, a bartender might use fermented pineapple juice in a Daiquiri or add fermented ginger to a Moscow Mule.

Another real-life example of the future of classic cocktails is the use of unusual flavor combinations. Bartenders and mixologists are constantly pushing the boundaries of what is possible with flavor, and are experimenting with unexpected combinations of ingredients to create new and exciting drinks. For example, a bartender might use smoked salt in a Margarita or add a hint of lavender to a Gin and Tonic.

In conclusion, the future of classic cocktails is an exciting and rapidly evolving landscape, with trends and innovations that are shaping the world of mixology. From the use of sustainable and locally sourced ingredients to the incorporation of technology and health and wellness benefits, there is a lot to look forward to in the world of cocktails. By pushing the boundaries of what is possible and exploring new and unexpected flavor combinations, bartenders and mixologists are able to create a truly memorable drinking experience for their customers.

CONCLUSION

Classic cocktails have stood the test of time for a reason. They are not only delicious, but they tell a story and evoke a sense of history and tradition. In this book, we have explored the rich history and art of classic cocktails, from their humble beginnings in speakeasies to their continued popularity today. We have delved into the techniques and tools of mixology, and shared tips and tricks to help you create the perfect cocktail.

We've explored the classics, from the Old Fashioned to the Whiskey Sour, and shown you how to put your own twist on these timeless recipes. We've also explored the future of classic cocktails, and how they will continue to evolve and adapt to changing tastes and trends. Throughout this book, we've emphasized the importance of quality ingredients and presentation.

We hope that this book has inspired you to explore the fascinating world of classic cocktails and develop your own skills as a mixologist. We encourage you to experiment with different recipes, ingredients, and techniques, and to continue to learn and grow in your appreciation for this timeless art form. As we raise a glass to the art of classic cocktails, we offer our gratitude to the bartenders, mixologists, and enthusiasts who have kept this tradition alive for over a century. Here's to the next hundred years of classic cocktails, and the endless creativity and innovation they will continue to inspire. Cheers!

BOOK 3
SMOKED COCKTAILS

INTRODUCTION

Mixology has come a long way, and the quest for new and exciting flavor combinations is constantly driving mixologists to explore innovative techniques. Smoking cocktails is one of those techniques that has captured the imagination of cocktail enthusiasts and mixologists alike. Smoked cocktails, with their complex and nuanced flavors, offer a sensory experience that is unmatched by any other technique.

In this book, we delve into the world of smoked cocktails, starting with the history of smoky drinks and how they have evolved over time. From the classic Mezcal-based cocktails to modern interpretations using ingredients like tea, herbs, and even fruitwood, we cover it all.

We also explore the science behind smoke-infused flavors and how different types of wood can affect the taste and aroma of a drink. We provide a comprehensive guide to the different smoking methods, from using a handheld smoker to using a smoke box, so you can choose the best technique for your needs.

But the heart of the book is the collection of mouth-watering recipes that showcase the art of smoked cocktails. We have included recipes for classic cocktails like the Old Fashioned and the Manhattan, as well as new creations like the Smoky Negroni and the Smoked Cherry Blossom. Each recipe is accompanied by expert tips and step-by-step instructions, so you can recreate these delicious drinks at home and impress your guests.

In addition to the recipes, we also provide guidance on selecting the right glassware, garnishes, and serving techniques to elevate your cocktail experience. We even offer suggestions for pairing smoked cocktails with food, so you can take your taste buds on a journey.

Whether you are a seasoned mixologist or a home bartender looking to up your game, this book is the ultimate guide to creating innovative, delicious, and unforgettable smoked cocktails. So grab a glass, fire up the smoker, and let's get started!

SMOKED COCKTAILS 101

When it comes to smoked cocktails, there's more than meets the eye. Behind every expertly crafted smoky libation lies a rich history and evolution that has taken place over centuries. In this chapter, we'll dive into the fascinating origins of smoked cocktails, exploring how this technique has evolved and adapted to various regions and cultures. We'll examine classic cocktails that have stood the test of time, and modern interpretations that push the boundaries of what's possible.

HISTORY OF SMOKED COCKTAILS

Cocktail culture has seen many trends come and go, but one of the most enduring and exciting developments of the past decade has been the rise of the smoked cocktail. These drinks add a new dimension to classic cocktails, bringing a smoky depth and complexity that is both intriguing and delicious. But where did this trend originate, and how did it become so popular? In this chapter, we'll take a deep dive into the origins of smoked cocktails and explore how this trend has evolved over time.

The use of smoke in cocktails is not a new concept. In fact, the practice of smoking drinks can be traced back to pre-prohibition times, when bartenders would use smoke to add flavor to their creations. One of the earliest recorded examples of a smoked cocktail is the "Smoky Martini," which was created by bartender Eben Freeman at Tailor, a New York City cocktail bar that opened in 2007.

The Smoky Martini was made by first smoking the glass with hickory chips, then adding gin and vermouth that had also been infused with smoke. This technique added a subtle smoky flavor to the classic martini, creating a new and exciting variation on a beloved classic.

Over time, other bartenders began experimenting with smoked cocktails, incorporating different types of wood chips, herbs, and spices to create unique flavor profiles. Some bartenders even started using actual smoke in their drinks, rather than just infusing the liquor with smoke beforehand.

While smoked cocktails had been around for years, it wasn't until the mid-2010s that they really started to gain mainstream popularity. This was due in large part to the growing interest in craft cocktails and the rise of the "speakeasy" style bar. These bars, which emphasized handcrafted cocktails made with high-quality ingredients, were the perfect setting for the smoked cocktail trend to take off. Bartenders began incorporating smoke into their drinks in increasingly creative ways, using everything from hand-held smokers to glass domes and even blow torches to achieve the perfect smoky flavor.

Today, smoked cocktails can be found at bars and restaurants all over the world, from high-end establishments to more casual spots. The trend has also inspired home bartenders to experiment with smoking their own cocktails, using everything from stovetop smokers to smoking guns to achieve the desired effect.

So, what does the future hold for smoked cocktails? While it's impossible to predict the next big trend in cocktail culture, it's clear that smoked cocktails are here to stay. Bartenders will continue to experiment with different types of smoke and flavor combinations, pushing the boundaries of what is possible with this technique. One area of potential growth is the use of smoked cocktails in food pairings. Many bars and restaurants are already offering smoked cocktails alongside smoked meats and other dishes, creating a cohesive flavor profile that is both delicious and unique.

Another trend to watch is the use of smoke in non-alcoholic cocktails. As more people opt for low- or no-alcohol drinks, bartenders are exploring new ways to add flavor and depth to these creations. Smoke is a natural fit, as it adds complexity without relying on alcohol content.

REGIONAL VARIATIONS

The trend of smoked cocktails has taken the world by storm, with bartenders from all corners of the globe incorporating smoke into their creations. But while the technique of smoking cocktails is universal, the specific ingredients and flavors used vary greatly depending on the region. In this chapter, we'll explore some of the regional variations of smoked cocktails and the unique flavors they bring to the table.

North America

North America is where the trend of smoked cocktails first gained traction, and it's also where some of the most iconic smoked cocktail recipes can be found. One classic example is the "Smokey Negroni," which features mezcal instead of gin, giving the drink a smoky flavor that perfectly balances the bitter notes of the Campari and the sweetness of the vermouth.

Another popular North American smoked cocktail is the "Smoke and Mirrors," which was created by bartender Justin Taylor at Vancouver's Boulevard Kitchen and Oyster Bar. The drink features mezcal, elderflower liqueur, and grapefruit bitters, all smoked with applewood to create a complex and flavorful cocktail.

South America

South America is known for its love of smoky flavors, so it's no surprise that the trend of smoked cocktails has taken off in this region as well. In Argentina, the "Smoky Mary" is a popular variation of the classic Bloody Mary, featuring a smoky tomato juice base made with charred tomatoes and smoked paprika.

In Brazil, the "Caipirinha Ahumada" is a smoky take on the classic caipirinha cocktail. Made with smoked cachaca, lime, and sugar, this cocktail packs a punch of smoky flavor with a refreshing citrus kick.

Europe

In Europe, smoked cocktails often incorporate regional ingredients to create unique flavor profiles. In Spain, for example, the "Smoked Gin Tonic" is a popular variation of the classic G&T. This drink features gin that has been infused with smoked tea leaves and is garnished with citrus and juniper berries.

In Italy, the "Smoked Negroni Sbagliato" is a twist on the classic Negroni, made with sparkling wine instead of gin. The drink is then smoked with cherrywood chips to add a subtle smoky flavor that complements the bitter and sweet notes of the drink.

Asia

In Asia, bartenders are experimenting with a variety of smoky flavors, from tea and spices to smoked fruits and vegetables. In Japan, the "Smoked Yuzu Sour" is a popular cocktail featuring yuzu juice, shochu, and smoked salt. The drink is then garnished with a smoked shiso leaf, which adds an additional layer of smoky flavor to the drink.

In India, the "Smoked Masala Chai" is a spiced tea cocktail that is smoked with a variety of aromatic spices, including cinnamon, cardamom, and cloves. The drink is then mixed with rum and served hot, creating a warm and comforting cocktail that is perfect for cool evenings.

CLASSIC SMOKED COCKTAILS

The trend of smoked cocktails has brought a new dimension to classic cocktail recipes, adding a depth and complexity that is both intriguing and delicious. But while there are countless variations of smoked cocktails out there, some classic recipes have stood the test of time. In this chapter, we'll explore some of the most iconic classic smoked cocktails and the unique flavors they bring to the table.

- **Smoked Old Fashioned:** The Old Fashioned is one of the most iconic cocktails of all time, and the smoked variation adds an extra layer of complexity to this beloved drink. To make a smoked Old Fashioned, start by smoking a glass with hickory chips. Then, in a separate glass, muddle a sugar cube, a few dashes of Angostura bitters, and a splash of water. Add ice and 2 oz of bourbon or rye whiskey, and stir until well chilled. Strain the drink into the smoked glass, and garnish with a smoked orange twist.

- **Smoked Manhattan:** The Manhattan is another classic cocktail that is elevated by the addition of smoke. To make a smoked Manhattan, start by smoking a mixing glass with cherrywood chips. Add ice to the smoked glass, and then add 2 oz of rye whiskey, 1 oz of sweet vermouth, and a few dashes of Angostura bitters. Stir until well chilled, then strain the drink into a fresh glass. Garnish with a smoked cherry.

- **Smokey Negroni:** The Negroni is a classic Italian cocktail that is traditionally made with gin, Campari, and sweet vermouth. The Smokey Negroni, however, uses mezcal instead of gin to give the drink a smoky flavor that perfectly balances the bitter and sweet notes of the drink. To make a Smokey Negroni, combine 1 oz of mezcal, 1 oz of Campari, and 1 oz of sweet vermouth in a mixing glass with ice. Stir until well chilled, then strain the drink into a glass filled with ice. Garnish with an orange twist.

- **Smoked Margarita:** The Margarita is a classic tequila cocktail that is often associated with tropical flavors and summer parties. The addition of smoke to this cocktail, however, gives it a deeper and more complex flavor profile that is perfect for cooler evenings. To make a Smoked Margarita, start by smoking a glass with hickory chips. In a separate glass, combine 2 oz of tequila, 1 oz of lime juice, and 1/2 oz of agave nectar. Add ice and stir until well chilled. Strain the drink into the smoked glass, and garnish with a smoked lime wedge.

- **Smoked Bloody Mary:** The Bloody Mary is a classic brunch cocktail that is known for its bold and spicy flavors. Adding smoke to this drink gives it a unique twist that is perfect for those who love smoky flavors. To make a Smoked Bloody Mary, start by smoking tomato juice with hickory chips. In a separate glass, combine 2 oz of vodka, 4 oz of the smoked tomato juice, and a splash of Worcestershire sauce. Add ice and stir until well chilled. Garnish with a smoked bacon strip and a celery stick.

MODERN INTERPRETATIONS

As the trend of smoked cocktails has grown in popularity, bartenders have become increasingly creative in their approach to incorporating smoke into their drinks. From using unusual ingredients to experimenting with new techniques, the world of modern smoked cocktails is full of exciting and unexpected twists on classic recipes. In this chapter, we'll explore some of the most innovative and intriguing modern interpretations of smoked cocktails.

- **Smoked Espresso Martini:** The Espresso Martini is a classic cocktail that combines coffee and vodka for a caffeinated kick. The addition of smoke to this drink gives it a new level of complexity and depth. To make a Smoked Espresso Martini, start by smoking coffee beans with hickory chips. In a shaker, combine 2 oz of vodka, 1 oz of coffee liqueur, and 1 oz of freshly brewed smoked espresso. Shake with ice, and strain into a chilled glass. Garnish with a smoked coffee bean.

- **Smoked Pineapple Margarita:** The Margarita is a classic tequila cocktail that is often associated with citrus and tropical flavors. The addition of smoked pineapple to this drink gives it a sweet and smoky twist. To make a Smoked Pineapple Margarita, start by smoking fresh pineapple with mesquite chips. In a shaker, combine 2 oz of tequila, 1 oz of lime juice, 1 oz of smoked pineapple juice, and 1/2 oz of agave nectar. Shake with ice, and strain into a glass filled with ice. Garnish with a smoked pineapple wedge.

- **Smoked Bloody Caesar:** The Bloody Caesar is a Canadian twist on the classic Bloody Mary, featuring clam juice and a variety of spices. The addition of smoke to this drink takes it to a whole new level of flavor. To make a Smoked Bloody Caesar, start by smoking tomato juice with applewood chips. In a shaker, combine 2 oz of vodka, 4 oz of the smoked tomato juice, 1 oz of clam juice, and a variety of spices, such as Worcestershire sauce, hot sauce, and celery salt. Shake with ice, and strain into a glass filled with ice. Garnish with a smoked clam or a smoked shrimp.

- **Smoked Maple Old Fashioned:** The Old Fashioned is a classic cocktail that is often associated with the flavors of bourbon and bitters. The addition of smoked maple syrup to this drink adds a sweet and smoky twist that perfectly complements the traditional flavors. To make a Smoked Maple Old Fashioned, start by smoking maple syrup with cherrywood chips. In a glass, muddle a sugar cube with a few dashes of Angostura bitters and a splash of water. Add ice and 2 oz of bourbon, and stir until well chilled. Strain the drink into a glass filled with ice, and drizzle the smoked maple syrup over the top. Garnish with a smoked orange twist.

- **Smoked Lemon Gin Fizz:** The Gin Fizz is a classic cocktail that is light and refreshing, making it perfect for summer sipping. The addition of smoke to this drink gives it a new level of complexity and depth. To make a Smoked Lemon Gin Fizz, start by smoking lemon juice with hickory chips. In a shaker, combine 2 oz of gin, 1 oz of smoked lemon juice, 1/2 oz of simple syrup, and a splash of soda water. Shake with ice, and strain into a glass filled with ice. Garnish with a smoked lemon slice.

The Science Behind Smoke-Infused Flavors

Have you ever wondered how smoked cocktails get their rich and complex flavors? The secret lies in the science behind smoke-infused flavors. In this chapter, we'll explore the impact of different types of wood on the taste and aroma of a drink, as well as the chemistry behind the smoke and alcohol reaction. We'll also delve into the art of combining flavors with smoke, giving you a deeper understanding of the magic that goes into creating the perfect smoked cocktail.

THE CHEMISTRY OF SMOKE AND ALCOHOL

When smoke and alcohol are combined in a cocktail, a complex chemical reaction takes place that can greatly impact the flavor and aroma of the drink. In this chapter, we'll explore the chemistry of smoke and alcohol, and how these two elements interact to create a delicious and complex smoked cocktail.

Smoke is a complex mixture of gases and particles that are produced when wood is burned. The main components of smoke are carbon monoxide, carbon dioxide, water vapor, and a range of organic compounds, including aldehydes, ketones, and phenols. When wood is burned, the heat breaks down the cellulose and hemicellulose in the wood, producing a range of volatile organic compounds (VOCs) that are released into the smoke. These VOCs are what give smoke its characteristic flavor and aroma.

Alcohol is a type of organic compound that is produced by the fermentation of sugar or starch. The main types of alcohol used in cocktails are ethanol and methanol. Ethanol is the type of alcohol that is consumed in alcoholic beverages and is responsible for the intoxicating effects of alcohol. When alcohol is consumed, it is metabolized by the liver into acetaldehyde and then into acetic acid. This process is known as alcohol metabolism and is responsible for the hangover symptoms that many people experience after drinking alcohol.

When smoke and alcohol are combined in a cocktail, a complex chemical reaction takes place. The organic compounds in the smoke can react with the alcohol, creating new compounds and changing the flavor and aroma of the drink. The aldehydes and phenols in the smoke can react with the ethanol in the alcohol, creating new compounds that can impart a range of flavors and aromas to the cocktail. For example, the smoky flavor of hickory wood can react with the vanilla notes in bourbon, creating a rich and complex flavor profile. The amount of smoke used can also impact the chemical reaction that takes place. A heavier smoke can produce more organic compounds, resulting in a stronger smoky flavor in the cocktail. However, too much smoke can overpower the other flavors in the drink, so it's important to find the right balance.

THE IMPACT OF WOOD ON FLAVOR AND AROMA

One of the key ingredients in creating a smoked cocktail is the wood used for smoking. The type of wood can greatly impact the flavor and aroma of the final drink, making it an important consideration for bartenders and home mixologists alike. In this chapter, we'll explore the impact of wood on flavor and aroma in smoked cocktails, and how different woods can be used to create unique and delicious drinks.

Types of Wood for Smoking Cocktails

There are many different types of wood that can be used for smoking cocktails, each with its own unique flavor profile. Some of the most popular woods used for smoking include:

- **Hickory** - This wood is known for its strong, smoky flavor and is often used for smoking meats. When used in cocktails, hickory can add a deep, rich smoky flavor that is perfect for darker spirits like bourbon and rye.
- **Mesquite** - This wood is commonly used for smoking meats in the southern United States and has a distinct, earthy flavor. When used in cocktails, mesquite can add a bold and smoky flavor that pairs well with tequila and mezcal.
- **Applewood** - This wood has a milder flavor than hickory or mesquite and is often used for smoking fish and poultry. When used in cocktails, applewood can add a subtle smoky flavor that is perfect for lighter spirits like gin and vodka.
- **Cherrywood** - This wood has a sweet, fruity flavor and is often used for smoking pork and poultry. When used in cocktails, cherrywood can add a subtle sweetness that pairs well with whiskey and rum.
- **Oak** - This wood is often used for aging spirits, as it imparts a woody, vanilla flavor. When used for smoking cocktails, oak can add a subtle smoky flavor with a hint of sweetness.

The type of wood used for smoking can greatly impact the flavor and aroma of a cocktail. In addition to the specific flavor of the wood, the amount of smoke used can also affect the final result. A heavier smoke will produce a stronger smoky flavor, while a lighter smoke will produce a more subtle flavor. The flavor and aroma of the wood can also vary depending on the age and moisture content of the wood. Dry wood will produce a stronger, more concentrated smoke flavor, while wet wood will produce a milder flavor.

Different woods can be used to enhance or complement the flavors of specific spirits. For example, the bold and smoky flavor of mesquite pairs well with tequila and mezcal, while the subtle sweetness of cherrywood complements the flavors of whiskey and rum. When smoking cocktails, it's important to consider the overall flavor profile of the drink and how the smoke will impact it. A smoky flavor can add depth and complexity to a cocktail, but too much smoke can overpower the other flavors in the drink.

DIFFERENT TYPES OF WOOD AND THEIR CHARACTERISTICS

Different types of wood have their own unique characteristics and flavor profiles, making them an important consideration for bartenders and home mixologists alike. In this chapter, we'll explore some of the most popular types of wood used for smoking cocktails and their specific characteristics. In this chapter, we'll take a deeper look at some of the most popular types of wood used for smoking cocktails, their specific characteristics, and the types of drinks they can be used with.

Hickory

Hickory wood is known for its strong, smoky flavor and is a popular choice for smoking cocktails. Hickory wood is harvested from the hickory tree and is known for its density and hardness. The wood has a sweet and slightly bitter taste that can also complement the flavors of spicy or sweet cocktails. Hickory wood can add a deep, rich smoky flavor that pairs well with darker spirits like bourbon and rye. Examples of drinks that can be made with hickory wood:

- **Smoked Old Fashioned:** This classic cocktail is made with bourbon or rye whiskey, sugar, bitters, and a smoked orange twist.

- **Smoked Manhattan:** This classic cocktail is made with rye whiskey, sweet vermouth, and bitters, with a smoked cherry garnish.

Mesquite

Mesquite wood is known for its earthy, smoky flavor and is commonly used for smoking meats. When used for smoking cocktails, mesquite can add a bold and smoky flavor that pairs well with tequila and mezcal. The wood has a slightly sweet taste and aroma that can also complement the flavors of citrus and spicy cocktails. Examples of drinks that can be made with mesquite wood:

- **Smoked Pineapple Margarita:** This cocktail is made with tequila, smoked pineapple juice, lime juice, and agave nectar, with a smoked pineapple wedge garnish.
- **Smokey Negroni:** This cocktail is made with mezcal, Campari, and sweet vermouth, with an orange twist garnish.

Applewood

Applewood is a milder wood that is often used for smoking fish and poultry. The wood is harvested from apple trees and is known for its sweet, fruity flavor. When used for smoking cocktails, applewood can add a subtle smoky flavor that pairs well with lighter spirits like gin and vodka. The wood has a light and slightly sweet taste that can also complement the flavors of fruit and herbal cocktails. Examples of drinks that can be made with applewood:

- **Smoked Lemon Gin Fizz:** This cocktail is made with gin, smoked lemon juice, simple syrup, and soda water, with a smoked lemon slice garnish.
- **Smoked Apple Martini:** This cocktail is made with vodka, smoked apple juice, and a splash of vermouth, with a smoked apple slice garnish.

Cherrywood

Cherrywood is harvested from cherry trees and is known for its sweet, fruity flavor. The wood has a reddish color and a dense, hardwood texture. When used for smoking cocktails, cherrywood can add a subtle sweetness that pairs well with whiskey and rum. The wood has a light, fruity taste and aroma that can also complement the flavors of citrus and spice cocktails. Examples of drinks that can be made with cherrywood:

- Smoked Maple Old Fashioned: This cocktail is made with bourbon, smoked maple syrup, bitters, and a cherrywood-smoked orange twist garnish.
- Smoked Cherry Manhattan: This cocktail is made with rye whiskey, sweet vermouth, and bitters, with a smoked cherry garnish.

Oak

Oak is a popular wood used for aging spirits, as it imparts a woody, vanilla flavor. When used for smoking cocktails, oak can add a subtle smoky flavor with a hint of sweetness. The wood has a dense, hardwood texture and a slightly bitter taste. Oak can complement the flavors of a variety of cocktails, from whiskey and rum to fruit and herbal drinks. Examples of drinks that can be made with oak:

- Smoked Vanilla Old Fashioned: This cocktail is made with bourbon, smoked vanilla syrup, bitters, and a smoked oak cube garnish.
- Smoked Pineapple Whiskey Sour: This cocktail is made with whiskey, smoked pineapple juice, lemon juice, and simple syrup, with a smoked oak chip garnish.

SMOKING TECHNIQUES & THEIR EFFECTS

Smoking techniques are an important aspect of creating a delicious and complex smoked cocktail. Different smoking techniques can be used to impart a range of flavors and aromas to the drink, making it an important consideration for bartenders and home mixologists alike. In this chapter, we'll explore some of the most popular smoking techniques and their effects on the final drink. There are several different smoking techniques that can be used to smoke cocktails, including:

Cold Smoking

Cold smoking is a technique that involves smoking the cocktail ingredients at a low temperature, usually between 68-86°F (20-30°C), for a longer period of time. This technique is often used to infuse the ingredients with a smoky flavor without changing their texture or cooking them. Cold smoking is typically done in a smokehouse or smoker using wood chips, sawdust, or pellets.

Hot Smoking

Hot smoking is a technique that involves smoking the cocktail ingredients at a higher temperature, usually between 176-212°F (80-100°C), for a shorter period of time. This technique is often used to cook and smoke the ingredients at the same time, infusing them with a rich, smoky flavor. Hot smoking is typically done on a grill, smoker, or stovetop using wood chips, chunks, or logs.

Smoking Gun

A smoking gun is a device that allows you to quickly and easily smoke cocktail ingredients. The device uses wood chips or sawdust and produces smoke that is blown into a sealed container with the ingredients. This technique is quick and efficient, and can be used to add a smoky flavor to a variety of cocktail ingredients.

Effects of Smoking Techniques

The smoking technique used can greatly impact the flavor and aroma of a smoked cocktail. Cold smoking is often used to infuse a subtle smoky flavor into the ingredients, while hot smoking can create a more intense and complex smoky flavor. The smoking gun technique can be used to add a quick and easy smoky flavor to a variety of cocktail ingredients. Different types of wood and smoking techniques can also be used to create a range of different flavors and aromas in smoked cocktails. For example, a hot smoke with mesquite wood can create a bold and earthy flavor, while a cold smoke with applewood can create a light and fruity flavor. The amount of smoke used can also impact the final flavor of the cocktail. A heavier smoke can produce a stronger smoky flavor, while a lighter smoke can produce a more subtle flavor. It's important to consider the overall flavor profile of the cocktail and how the smoke will impact it.

COMBINING FLAVORS WITH SMOKE

Combining flavors with smoke is an art form that can elevate a cocktail from ordinary to extraordinary. When done correctly, smoke can add a depth and complexity to the drink that enhances the other flavors and creates a unique and memorable experience for the drinker. In this chapter, we'll explore some tips for combining flavors with smoke to create delicious and complex smoked cocktails.

- **Consider the Spirit:** When combining flavors with smoke, it's important to consider the type of spirit being used in the cocktail. Different spirits have different flavor profiles and can pair well with different types of smoke. For example, a smoky, peated scotch can pair well with a bold and earthy smoke, while a light and fruity cocktail may pair better with a subtle applewood smoke.

- **Balance the Flavors:** When combining flavors with smoke, it's important to find a balance between the smoke and the other flavors in the drink. Too much smoke can overpower the other flavors and make the drink unbalanced, while too little smoke may not add enough depth and complexity to the drink. It's important to experiment with different amounts of smoke to find the right balance for each cocktail.

- **Use Fresh Ingredients:** Using fresh ingredients in a smoked cocktail is important to ensure that the flavors are at their peak. Fresh herbs, fruits, and juices can add a bright and vibrant flavor to the drink that pairs well with the smoky notes. It's also important to use high-quality spirits and mixers to ensure that the drink has a balanced flavor profile.

- **Experiment with Different Smoke Sources:** There are several different sources of smoke that can be used to flavor a cocktail, including wood chips, sawdust, and tea leaves. Each source of smoke has its own unique flavor profile and can be used to create different flavor combinations. It's important to experiment with different smoke sources to find the ones that pair well with the other flavors in the cocktail.

- **Use Smoke as a Garnish:** Smoke can also be used as a garnish in a smoked cocktail. This can be done by smoking a piece of fruit or herb and using it as a garnish on the rim of the glass. The smoke can add an extra layer of flavor to the drink and create a unique visual experience for the drinker.

Examples of Flavor Combinations with Smoke

- **Smoked Maple and Bourbon:** This cocktail is made with bourbon, smoked maple syrup, and bitters. The smoky notes of the wood complement the rich, sweet flavors of the maple syrup and bourbon, creating a complex and delicious drink.

- **Smoked Pineapple and Tequila:** This cocktail is made with tequila, smoked pineapple juice, lime juice, and agave nectar. The smoky notes of the wood complement the sweet and tangy flavors of the pineapple and lime, while the tequila adds a bold and earthy flavor.

- **Smoked Rosemary and Gin**: This cocktail is made with gin, smoked rosemary syrup, and lemon juice. The smoky notes of the rosemary complement the herbal and citrus flavors of the gin and lemon juice, creating a light and refreshing drink.

Smoking Techniques

The technique used to smoke cocktails can have a significant impact on the final product. From handheld smokers to smoke boxes, the options for smoking techniques are endless. In this chapter, we'll explore the different methods of smoking cocktails, including smoking with wood chips and herbs. We'll also discuss important safety precautions to keep in mind while smoking your drinks. So, whether you're a seasoned mixologist or a beginner, get ready to discover the art of smoking cocktails like a pro.

USING A HANDHELD SMOKER

A handheld smoker is a versatile tool that can be used to smoke cocktails, meats, fish, and more. This compact and portable device allows you to quickly and easily add a smoky flavor to your drinks without the need for a large smoker or grill. In this chapter, we'll explore how to use a handheld smoker to smoke cocktails and create delicious and complex drinks.

A handheld smoker is a small, battery-powered device that produces smoke to flavor food and drinks. The device consists of a chamber for wood chips or pellets, a fan to circulate the smoke, and a nozzle to direct the smoke where it is needed. The device can be used on a variety of foods and drinks, including cocktails, meats, fish, vegetables, and cheese. Using a handheld smoker to smoke cocktails is a simple process that can be done in a few easy steps:

1. **Choose the Wood Chips:** The first step is to choose the type of wood chips that you want to use for your cocktail. Different types of wood chips can produce different flavors and aromas, so it's important to choose the ones that will complement the other flavors in your drink.

2. **Prepare the Cocktail Ingredients:** Prepare the cocktail ingredients as you normally would, making sure that they are at room temperature. If you are using fresh herbs or fruit, make sure that they are washed and dried before use.

3. **Load the Handheld Smoker:** Load the handheld smoker with the wood chips, making sure to follow the manufacturer's instructions for your specific device.

4. **Smoke the Cocktail Ingredients:** Place the cocktail ingredients in a sealed container, such as a cocktail shaker or glass, and insert the nozzle of the handheld smoker into the container. Turn on the smoker and allow the smoke to circulate for a few seconds to a few minutes, depending on the desired intensity of the smoky flavor.

5. **Serve and Enjoy:** Remove the nozzle from the container and mix or strain the cocktail as you normally would. Serve the cocktail immediately and enjoy the delicious and complex smoky flavor.

Tips for Using a Handheld Smoker

Here are some tips for using a handheld smoker to smoke cocktails:

- **Choose the Right Wood Chips:** Choose wood chips that will complement the other flavors in your cocktail, such as applewood for fruity drinks or hickory for bold, spicy cocktails.

- **Use a Sealed Container:** Use a sealed container, such as a cocktail shaker or glass, to contain the smoke and ensure that the flavor is evenly distributed throughout the drink.

- **Control the Smoke Intensity:** The intensity of the smoky flavor can be controlled by adjusting the amount of time the ingredients are exposed to the smoke.

- **Experiment with Different Techniques:** Experiment with different smoking techniques, such as smoking the glassware or garnishes, to create a range of unique and delicious smoked cocktails.

Using a handheld smoker is a quick and easy way to add a smoky flavor to your cocktails. By choosing the right wood chips, using a sealed container, controlling the smoke intensity, and experimenting with different techniques, you can create a wide range of delicious and complex smoked cocktails that will impress any palate. With a little creativity and experimentation, the possibilities for using a handheld smoker are endless.

USING A SMOKE BOX

A smoke box is a device that consists of a chamber for wood chips, a fan to circulate the smoke, and a hose or tube to direct the smoke where it is needed. The smoke box can be used on a variety of foods and drinks, including cocktails, meats, fish, vegetables, and cheese. The smoke box is a convenient and portable tool that allows you to quickly add a smoky flavor to your cocktails without the need for a large smoker or grill. Using a smoke box to smoke cocktails is a simple process that can be done in a few easy steps:

1. **Choose the Wood Chips:** The first step is to choose the type of wood chips that you want to use for your cocktail. Different types of wood chips can produce different flavors and aromas, so it's important to choose the ones that will complement the other flavors in your drink.

2. **Prepare the Cocktail Ingredients:** Prepare the cocktail ingredients as you normally would, making sure that they are at room temperature. If you are using fresh herbs or fruit, make sure that they are washed and dried before use.

3. **Load the Smoke Box:** Load the smoke box with the wood chips, making sure to follow the manufacturer's instructions for your specific device.

4. **Smoke the Cocktail Ingredients:** Place the cocktail ingredients in a sealed container, such as a cocktail shaker or glass, and attach the hose or tube from the smoke box to the container. Turn on the smoke box and allow the smoke to circulate for a few seconds to a few minutes, depending on the desired intensity of the smoky flavor.

5. **Serve and Enjoy:** Remove the hose or tube from the container and mix or strain the cocktail as you normally would. Serve the cocktail immediately and enjoy the delicious and complex smoky flavor.

SMOKING WITH WOOD CHIPS

Smoking with wood chips is a popular method of adding a smoky flavor to cocktails. Wood chips can be used in a variety of smoking devices, including smokers, grills, and handheld smokers, to infuse cocktails with a delicious and complex smoky flavor. In this chapter, we'll explore how to smoke cocktails with wood chips and create delicious and unique drinks.

The first step in smoking cocktails with wood chips is choosing the right type of wood chips. Once you have chosen the type of wood chips, it's important to prepare them before smoking. Soak the wood chips in water for at least 30 minutes before using them. This will help the wood chips to smoke more slowly and evenly, allowing the smoky flavor to infuse the cocktail.

Using Wood Chips in a Smoker or Grill

If you have a smoker or grill, you can use wood chips to smoke your cocktails. Simply add the soaked wood chips to the smoker or grill and allow them to heat up until they start to smoke. Place the cocktail ingredients in a sealed container, such as a cocktail shaker or glass, and place the container in the smoker or grill. Allow the cocktail ingredients to smoke for a few minutes, then remove them from the smoker or grill and mix or strain the cocktail as you normally would.

Using Wood Chips in a Handheld Smoker

If you have a handheld smoker, you can use wood chips to smoke your cocktails as well. Simply load the handheld smoker with the soaked wood chips and place the nozzle of the smoker into the container with the cocktail ingredients. Turn on the smoker and allow the smoke to circulate for a few seconds to a few minutes, depending on the desired intensity of the smoky flavor. Remove the nozzle from the container and mix or strain the cocktail as you normally would.

Tips for Using Wood Chips

Here are some tips for using wood chips to smoke cocktails:

- **Use the Right Amount of Wood Chips:** Using too few wood chips will result in a weak smoky flavor, while using too many will overpower the other flavors in the cocktail.

- **Control the Smoke Intensity:** The intensity of the smoky flavor can be controlled by adjusting the amount of time the cocktail ingredients are exposed to the smoke.

- **Experiment with Different Combinations:** Experiment with different types of wood chips and combinations of wood chips to create unique and delicious smoky flavors.

- **Choose Fresh Ingredients:** Use fresh herbs, fruits, and juices to ensure that the flavors are at their peak and can stand up to the smoky flavor.

SMOKING WITH HERBS & SPICES

Smoking with herbs and spices is a technique that can add a new dimension of flavor to your cocktails. By using aromatic herbs and spices in combination with wood smoke, you can create complex and unique flavor profiles in your drinks. In this chapter, we'll explore how to smoke cocktails with herbs and spices and create delicious and distinctive drinks.

Choosing the Right Herbs and Spices: The first step in smoking cocktails with herbs and spices is choosing the right herbs and spices. Different herbs and spices can add different flavors and aromas to your cocktails, so it's important to choose the ones that will complement the other flavors in your drink. Here are some examples of herbs and spices and their flavors:

- **Rosemary:** Rosemary has a strong and woody flavor that pairs well with gin-based cocktails.

- **Thyme:** Thyme has a subtle and earthy flavor that pairs well with whiskey-based cocktails.

- **Cinnamon:** Cinnamon has a warm and spicy flavor that pairs well with rum-based cocktails.

- **Star Anise:** Star anise has a sweet and licorice-like flavor that pairs well with vodka-based cocktails.

Preparing the Herbs and Spices: Once you have chosen the herbs and spices, it's important to prepare them before smoking. Dry the herbs and spices thoroughly before smoking to avoid excessive moisture in the smoking process. You can also crush the herbs and spices to release more of their essential oils and aroma. Using a combination of dried and fresh herbs can also create more complex flavors.

Using Herbs and Spices in a Smoker or Grill

If you have a smoker or grill, you can use herbs and spices to smoke your cocktails. Simply add the herbs and spices to the smoker or grill along with the soaked wood chips and allow them to heat up until they start to smoke. Place the cocktail ingredients in a sealed container, such as a cocktail shaker or glass, and place the container in the smoker or grill. Allow the cocktail ingredients to smoke for a few minutes, then remove them from the smoker or grill and mix or strain the cocktail as you normally would.

Using Herbs and Spices in a Handheld Smoker

If you have a handheld smoker, you can use herbs and spices to smoke your cocktails as well. Simply load the handheld smoker with the herbs and spices and place the nozzle of the smoker into the container with the cocktail ingredients. Turn on the smoker and allow the smoke to circulate for a few seconds to a few minutes, depending on the desired intensity of the smoky flavor. Remove the nozzle from the container and mix or strain the cocktail as you normally would.

Tips for Using Herbs and Spices

Here are some tips for using herbs and spices to smoke cocktails:

- **Experiment with Different Combinations:** Experiment with different combinations of herbs and spices to create unique and delicious smoky flavors.

- **Use Fresh Ingredients:** Use fresh herbs, fruits, and juices to ensure that the flavors are at their peak and can stand up to the smoky flavor.

- **Choose Complementary Flavors:** Choose herbs and spices that will complement the other flavors in your cocktail, rather than overpowering them.

- **Crush the Herbs and Spices:** Crushing the herbs and spices can release more of their essential oils and aroma, creating a more intense flavor.

SAFETY PRECAUTIONS FOR SMOKING COCKTAILS

Smoking cocktails can be a fun and creative way to add a unique and delicious flavor to your drinks. However, it's important to take certain safety precautions to ensure that the process is safe and enjoyable. In this chapter, we'll explore some of the key safety precautions that you should take when smoking cocktails.

- **Work in a Well-Ventilated Area:** When smoking cocktails, it's important to work in a well-ventilated area. This will help to dissipate the smoke and prevent it from becoming too concentrated, which can be hazardous to your health. Open windows and doors to provide a good airflow and avoid inhaling the smoke directly.

- **Use a Smoke Box or Handheld Smoker:** Using a smoke box or handheld smoker can help to contain the smoke and prevent it from spreading throughout your home or bar. This will help to keep the smoke from getting into your eyes or lungs, and will also prevent the smoke from setting off fire alarms.

- **Use Safety Equipment:** When working with smoke, it's important to use safety equipment such as gloves and eye protection. This will help to protect your hands and eyes from the smoke and any debris that may be produced during the smoking process.

- **Keep Flammable Materials Away:** Smoking cocktails can produce a lot of heat and smoke, so it's important to keep flammable materials away from the smoking area. This includes paper, cloth, and any other materials that can easily catch fire. It's also a good idea to have a fire extinguisher nearby, just in case.

- **Follow Manufacturer's Instructions:** When using a smoke box or handheld smoker, it's important to follow the manufacturer's instructions. This will ensure that you are using the device safely and effectively, and will also help to prevent any accidents or injuries.

- **Don't Overdo It:** It's important to remember that smoking cocktails is a technique that should be used in moderation. Over-smoking your cocktails can result in a flavor that is too strong or overpowering, and can also be hazardous to your health. Start with a small amount of smoke and gradually increase the intensity until you achieve the desired flavor.

With these safety precautions in mind, you can experiment with different smoking techniques and create a wide range of delicious and complex smoked cocktails that will impress any palate.

The Art of Smoked Cocktails

Creating the perfect smoked cocktail is more than just adding smoke to a drink. It's an art that requires a careful consideration of glassware, garnishes, ice, and even the way you shake or stir a drink. In this chapter, we'll delve into the art of smoked cocktails, exploring the nuances that elevate a good drink to a great one. We'll guide you through selecting the right glassware, choosing the perfect garnish, and understanding the importance of ice. We'll also discuss the pros and cons of stirring vs. shaking, as well as the etiquette of sipping vs. shooting. So, get ready to become a master mixologist and impress your guests with the art of smoked cocktails. Grab a glass, and let's begin.

SELECTING THE RIGHT GLASSWARE

When it comes to smoked cocktails, selecting the right glassware can have a significant impact on the presentation and enjoyment of the drink. The right glassware can enhance the aromas and flavors of the smoke and create a more sophisticated drinking experience. In this chapter, we'll explore some of the key factors to consider when selecting the right glassware for smoked cocktails.

- **Size and Shape:** The size and shape of the glassware can greatly affect the overall drinking experience. Larger glasses with wider rims allow the smoke to circulate more freely, which can enhance the aroma and flavor of the smoke. Conversely, smaller glasses with narrower rims can trap the smoke, creating a more concentrated and intense smoky flavor.

- **Material:** The material of the glassware can also have an impact on the drinking experience. Glassware made from crystal or other high-quality materials can enhance the visual and tactile experience of the drink, while plastic or other cheap materials can detract from it. It is always recommended to use glassware made from high-quality materials when serving smoked cocktails.

- **Stem or No Stem:** The decision to use stemmed or stemless glassware is a matter of personal preference. Stemmed glasses are more traditional and can provide a more elegant and sophisticated presentation. However, stemless glasses are often more practical and can be more comfortable to hold. Ultimately, the decision should be based on the specific drink being served and the occasion.

- **Design:** The design of the glassware can also play a role in the overall presentation of the drink. Glasses with intricate designs or etchings can create a more unique and sophisticated appearance, while simpler designs can provide a more classic and understated look. The choice of design should be based on the specific drink being served and the overall aesthetic of the occasion.

- **Functionality:** Finally, the choice of glassware should be based on the functionality of the drink being served. Certain drinks may require specific glassware to properly showcase the ingredients and flavors, while others may be more flexible in terms of glassware. It's important to consider the functionality of the drink and select the appropriate glassware accordingly.

CHOOSING THE RIGHT GARNISHES

Garnishes are an essential part of any cocktail, and can add visual appeal, texture, and flavor to a drink. When it comes to smoked cocktails, choosing the right garnish can complement the smoky flavor and enhance the overall drinking experience. In this chapter, we'll explore some of the key factors to consider when selecting the right garnish for smoked cocktails.

- **Complementary Flavors:** The first and most important factor to consider when choosing a garnish for smoked cocktails is the complementary flavors. The garnish should enhance and complement the smoky flavor of the drink without overpowering it. For example, citrus fruits like orange, lemon or lime can provide a fresh and tangy contrast to the smoky flavor, while herbs like rosemary or thyme can add an earthy and aromatic note.

- **Aesthetic Appeal:** The garnish can also enhance the visual appeal of the cocktail. Choosing a garnish that matches the color of the cocktail or complements the glassware can create a more sophisticated and visually appealing drink. Garnishes like edible flowers, fruit peels, or spices can add a pop of color or texture to the drink and make it look more appetizing.

- **Practicality:** The choice of garnish should also be based on practicality. Some garnishes may require more time and effort to prepare or may not be readily available. It's important to select a garnish that is practical and easy to prepare, while also providing the desired flavor and aesthetic appeal.

- **Seasonality:** The seasonality of the garnish can also play a role in the selection process. Choosing a garnish that is in season can provide the freshest and most flavorful ingredient, while also adding a seasonal touch to the drink. For example, berries and stone fruits are a great garnish option in the summer, while cinnamon sticks and nutmeg are more appropriate in the fall.

- **Texture:** The texture of the garnish can also add a unique and interesting element to the drink. Crunchy garnishes like toasted nuts or crumbled cookies can provide a satisfying contrast to the smoothness of the cocktail, while soft garnishes like whipped cream or marshmallows can add a creamy and luxurious texture.

By selecting the appropriate garnish for each individual drink, you can enhance the smoky flavor and create a more sophisticated and enjoyable drinking experience that will impress any guest. With these tips in mind, you can experiment with different garnishes and create a wide range of delicious and complex smoked cocktails that will be a hit at any occasion.

UNDERSTANDING THE IMPORTANCE OF ICE

Ice is a crucial component of any cocktail, and can have a significant impact on the flavor and presentation of the drink. When it comes to smoked cocktails, ice can play an important role in balancing the smoky flavor and creating a more enjoyable drinking experience. In this chapter, we'll explore the importance of ice in smoked cocktails and how to use it effectively.

Dilution: One of the main functions of ice in cocktails is dilution. Dilution helps to balance the flavors of the drink and reduce the harshness of the alcohol. In smoked cocktails, the smoky flavor can be quite intense, so dilution is particularly important to create a more balanced and enjoyable drinking experience.

Temperature: Ice also helps to chill the drink, which can enhance the flavor and aroma. When the drink is served at the proper temperature, the flavors are more pronounced and the aromas are more prominent. This can enhance the smoky flavor and create a more complex and enjoyable drinking experience.

Size and Shape: The size and shape of the ice can also have an impact on the drink. Larger ice cubes melt more slowly, which can reduce the dilution and keep the drink cooler for longer. Smaller ice cubes melt more quickly, which can increase the dilution but can also add a more textured mouthfeel. The shape of the ice can also affect the presentation of the drink, with unique shapes like spheres or cubes adding a sophisticated and elegant touch.

Quality: The quality of the ice is also important in smoked cocktails. Impurities in the ice can affect the flavor and aroma of the drink, so it's important to use high-quality ice made from filtered water. Using ice that is free from impurities can ensure that the flavors and aromas of the smoky cocktail are not compromised.

Timing: Finally, the timing of adding ice to the cocktail is also important. Adding ice too early can lead to over-dilution, while adding it too late can lead to a drink that is too strong and lacks balance. It's important to add ice at the appropriate time to achieve the desired balance of flavors.

By using ice effectively, you can balance the smoky flavor and create a more enjoyable drinking experience. With these tips in mind, you can experiment with different ice sizes and shapes, and create a wide range of delicious and complex smoked cocktails that will impress any palate.

STIRRING VS. SHAKING

Stirring and shaking are two of the most common methods of mixing cocktails. Both techniques have their own advantages and can affect the flavor and texture of the drink in different ways. When it comes to smoked cocktails, the choice between stirring and shaking can have a significant impact on the overall drinking experience. In this chapter, we'll explore the differences between stirring and shaking for smoked cocktails and when to use each technique.

Stirring

Stirring is a gentle method of mixing cocktails that is typically used for drinks that are all spirit-based, such as martinis or manhattans. The goal of stirring is to chill the drink while minimizing dilution and maintaining the clarity of the cocktail. When it comes to smoked cocktails, stirring can help to balance the smoky flavor without introducing any additional air or dilution.

Advantages of Stirring:

- **Less Dilution** - Stirring is a gentler technique that introduces less water into the drink, which can help to preserve the flavor and texture of the cocktail.

- **Clarity** - Stirring is less likely to introduce air into the drink, which can help to maintain the clarity of the cocktail and keep the smoke separate from the other ingredients.

- **Smooth Texture** - Stirring can create a smoother texture than shaking, which can be more appropriate for certain cocktails.

Disadvantages of Stirring:

- **Slower** - Stirring takes longer than shaking, which can be a disadvantage in a busy bar environment.

- **Limited Flavor Mixing** - Stirring may not mix flavors as thoroughly as shaking, which can be a disadvantage for more complex cocktails.

Shaking

Shaking is a more vigorous method of mixing cocktails that is typically used for drinks that contain citrus or other ingredients that need to be mixed more thoroughly. The goal of shaking is to aerate the drink, which can add texture and enhance the flavors of the cocktail. When it comes to smoked cocktails, shaking can help to introduce the smoky flavor throughout the drink and create a more complex and layered taste.

Advantages of Shaking:

- **Flavor Mixing** - Shaking can mix the flavors of the cocktail more thoroughly, which can be an advantage for more complex drinks.

- **Texture** - Shaking can introduce air into the drink, which can create a frothy and more textured mouthfeel.

- **Faster** - Shaking is a faster method of mixing than stirring, which can be an advantage in a busy bar environment.

Disadvantages of Shaking:

- **More Dilution** - Shaking introduces more water into the drink than stirring, which can dilute the flavor of the cocktail.
- **Clarity** - Shaking can cloud the drink, which can be a disadvantage for cocktails that are meant to be clear or have distinct layers.

SIPPING VS. SHOOTING

Sipping and shooting are two different ways to consume cocktails, each with its own advantages and disadvantages. When it comes to smoked cocktails, the choice between sipping and shooting can greatly impact the drinking experience. In this chapter, we'll explore the differences between sipping and shooting for smoked cocktails and when to use each technique.

Sipping

Sipping is the more traditional and sophisticated way of consuming cocktails. Sipping is a slow and deliberate way of drinking, where the focus is on savoring the flavor and aroma of the drink. Smoked cocktails are often complex and flavorful, so sipping is an excellent way to fully experience the different layers of flavors and the smoky aroma. Sipping also allows the drink to slowly evolve as the ice melts and the flavors meld together.

Advantages of Sipping:

- **Full Flavor Experience** - Sipping allows the drinker to fully experience the different layers of flavors in the cocktail, including the smoky flavor.

- **Sophisticated** - Sipping is a more refined and sophisticated way of consuming cocktails, which can enhance the overall drinking experience.
- **Relaxing** - Sipping encourages a slower and more relaxed drinking pace, which can be more enjoyable for certain occasions.

Disadvantages of Sipping:

- **Time-Consuming** - Sipping takes longer than shooting, which can be a disadvantage in a busy bar environment.
- **Less Intense** - Sipping may result in a less intense flavor experience than shooting, which can be a disadvantage for those who prefer stronger flavors.

Shooting

Shooting is the more casual and faster way of consuming cocktails. Shooting involves quickly consuming the entire drink in one gulp, often with the goal of getting drunk quickly. While shooting is not usually recommended for complex cocktails like smoked cocktails, it can be appropriate for certain occasions or drinks that are meant to be consumed quickly.

Advantages of Shooting:

- **Quick** - Shooting is a faster way of consuming cocktails, which can be an advantage in a busy bar environment or for those in a hurry.
- **Stronger Flavor** - Shooting can result in a stronger and more intense flavor experience than sipping, which can be an advantage for those who prefer stronger flavors.

Disadvantages of Shooting:

- **Less Enjoyable** - Shooting is a less enjoyable way of consuming cocktails than sipping, as it doesn't allow the drinker to fully experience the different layers of flavors and the smoky aroma.

- **Less Sophisticated** - Shooting is a less refined and sophisticated way of consuming cocktails, which can detract from the overall drinking experience.

When it comes to smoked cocktails, sipping is often the more appropriate way to consume the drink, as it allows the drinker to fully experience the complex flavors and smoky aroma. Shooting is generally not recommended for complex cocktails like smoked cocktails, but can be appropriate for certain occasions or drinks that are meant to be consumed quickly. With these tips in mind, you can choose the appropriate consumption method for each individual drink and create a wide range of delicious and complex smoked cocktails that will impress any palate.

Pairing Smoked Cocktails with Food

Smoked cocktails are more than just a drink - they are a sensory experience that can be enhanced by pairing them with the right food. In this chapter, we'll explore the art of pairing smoked cocktails with food, from appetizers to desserts. We'll guide you through understanding the flavor profile of smoked cocktails, so you can select the perfect pairing for your next meal.

We'll also share tips on pairing smoked cocktails with appetizers, entrees, and desserts, giving you the knowledge and confidence to create unforgettable dining experiences. So, whether you're hosting a dinner party or just looking to elevate your next meal, get ready to discover the art of pairing smoked cocktails with food.

UNDERSTANDING THE FLAVOR PROFILE OF SMOKED COCKTAILS

Smoked cocktails have become increasingly popular in recent years, and for good reason. The smoky flavor can add a complex and unique element to the drink, creating a more enjoyable drinking experience. However, understanding the flavor profile of smoked cocktails can be a bit tricky, as there are many different factors that can affect the taste of the drink. In this chapter, we'll explore the key components of the flavor profile of smoked cocktails and how to balance them effectively.

- **Smoke Flavor:** The smoke flavor is the most important component of smoked cocktails. It is what makes the drink unique and adds a smoky, woodsy note to the cocktail. The smoke flavor can come from a variety of sources, such as wood chips, herbs, or spices. The type of wood or herb used can greatly impact the flavor of the cocktail, as can the method of smoking.

- **Sweetness:** Sweetness is another important component of smoked cocktails. Sweetness can help to balance the smoky flavor and provide a more pleasant drinking experience. Common sweeteners used in smoked cocktails include honey, maple syrup, or simple syrup. The amount of sweetness used will depend on the individual taste preference of the drinker.

- **Sourness:** Sourness is another important component of smoked cocktails. Sourness can provide a tart and refreshing contrast to the smoky flavor. Common sour ingredients used in smoked cocktails include lemon or lime juice. The amount of sourness used will depend on the individual taste preference of the drinker.

- **Bitterness:** Bitterness can add a complex and sophisticated element to smoked cocktails. Common bitter ingredients used in smoked cocktails include bitters or amaros. Bitterness can help to balance the sweetness and add depth to the flavor profile of the cocktail.

- **Aromatics:** Aromatics are the final component of the flavor profile of smoked cocktails. Aromatics can add an herbal or floral note to the drink and enhance the overall drinking experience. Common aromatic ingredients used in smoked cocktails include herbs like rosemary or thyme, or spices like cinnamon or nutmeg.

PAIRING SMOKED COCKTAILS WITH APPETIZERS

Pairing smoked cocktails with appetizers can greatly enhance the overall dining experience. The smoky flavor in the cocktail can complement and elevate the flavors in the appetizer, creating a more enjoyable and satisfying dining experience. In this chapter, we'll explore some tips for pairing smoked cocktails with appetizers and provide some delicious pairing ideas.

Consider the Flavor Profile: When pairing smoked cocktails with appetizers, it's important to consider the flavor profile of both the cocktail and the appetizer. Look for complementary flavors and textures that will enhance each other. For example, a smoky and savory cocktail may pair well with an appetizer that is also smoky and savory, such as bacon-wrapped dates or grilled shrimp skewers.

Pair with the Occasion: Consider the occasion or event when pairing smoked cocktails with appetizers. For a more casual event, such as a backyard barbecue, you may want to pair a smoky cocktail with a hearty appetizer, such as pulled pork sliders. For a more formal event, such as a dinner party, you may want to pair a smoky cocktail with a more elegant appetizer, such as smoked salmon crostini.

Balance the Strength: When pairing smoked cocktails with appetizers, it's important to balance the strength of both the cocktail and the appetizer. A strong and bold cocktail may overpower a delicate appetizer, while a mild cocktail may be overshadowed by a strong and flavorful appetizer. For example, a smoky and bold cocktail may pair well with a spicy appetizer, such as buffalo wings, while a lighter and more delicate cocktail may pair well with a mild and creamy appetizer, such as brie and crackers.

Contrast the Flavors: Another way to pair smoked cocktails with appetizers is to contrast the flavors. This can create a more interesting and complex dining experience. For example, a smoky and savory cocktail may pair well with a sweet and fruity appetizer, such as fig and prosciutto skewers. The sweetness of the appetizer can contrast the smoky flavor of the cocktail, creating a more interesting and enjoyable flavor experience.

Pairing Ideas:

- Smoky Old Fashioned paired with bacon-wrapped dates
- Mezcal Margarita paired with grilled shrimp skewers
- Smoked Bloody Mary paired with deviled eggs
- Smoked Whiskey Sour paired with pulled pork sliders
- Smoky Negroni paired with smoked salmon crostini
- Smoked Manhattan paired with charcuterie board
- Smoked Martinez paired with smoked Gouda cheese
- Smoky Spiced Rum paired with jerk chicken skewers
- Smoked Gin and Tonic paired with prosciutto-wrapped melon
- Smoky Mezcal Mule paired with spicy guacamole and tortilla chips.

PAIRING SMOKED COCKTAILS WITH ENTREES

Pairing smoked cocktails with entrees is a delicious and unique way to enhance the dining experience. The smoky flavor in the cocktail can complement and elevate the flavors in the entree, creating a more enjoyable and satisfying meal. In this chapter, we'll explore some tips for pairing smoked cocktails with entrees and provide some authentic pairing ideas.

Consider the Flavor Profile: When pairing smoked cocktails with entrees, it's essential to consider the flavor profile of both the cocktail and the entree. Look for complementary flavors and textures that will enhance each other. For example, a smoky and spicy cocktail may pair well with an entree that is also spicy and smoky, such as a spicy barbecue rib or smoky brisket.

Pair with the Occasion: The occasion is crucial when pairing smoked cocktails with entrees. For a casual event, such as a backyard barbecue, you may want to pair a smoky cocktail with a hearty entree, such as grilled steak or smoked chicken. For a more formal event, such as a dinner party, you may want to pair a smoky cocktail with a more elegant entree, such as roasted pork tenderloin or grilled salmon.

Balance the Strength: When pairing smoked cocktails with entrees, it's crucial to balance the strength of both the cocktail and the entree. A strong and bold cocktail may overpower a delicate entree, while a mild cocktail may be overshadowed by a strong and flavorful entree. For example, a smoky and bold cocktail may pair well with a spicy and bold entree, such as spicy shrimp pasta, while a lighter and more delicate cocktail may pair well with a mild and creamy entree, such as mushroom risotto.

Contrast the Flavors: Contrasting flavors is an excellent way to pair smoked cocktails with entrees. It creates a more complex and exciting dining experience. For example, a smoky and spicy cocktail may pair well with a sweet and fruity entree, such as grilled peaches and pork chops. The sweetness of the entree can contrast the smoky and spicy flavor of the cocktail, creating a more interesting and enjoyable flavor experience.

Pairing Ideas:

- Smoky Mezcal Margarita paired with spicy barbecue ribs
- Smoked Old Fashioned paired with grilled steak and mushrooms
- Smoky Bloody Mary paired with smoked brisket and cornbread
- Smoked Whiskey Sour paired with roasted pork tenderloin and sweet potato mash
- Smoky Negroni paired with grilled salmon and asparagus
- Smoked Manhattan paired with braised lamb shanks and polenta
- Smoked Martinez paired with smoked duck breast and roasted root vegetables
- Smoky Spiced Rum paired with jerk chicken and grilled pineapple
- Smoked Gin and Tonic paired with grilled vegetables and quinoa salad
- Smoky Mezcal Mule paired with mushroom risotto and truffle oil.

PAIRING SMOKED COCKTAILS WITH DESSERTS

Pairing smoked cocktails with desserts is an exciting and unexpected way to elevate your dining experience. The smoky flavor in the cocktail can complement and enhance the flavors in the dessert, creating a unique and memorable taste sensation. In this chapter, we'll explore some tips for pairing smoked cocktails with desserts and provide some authentic pairing ideas.

Consider the Flavor Profile: When pairing smoked cocktails with desserts, it's important to consider the flavor profile of both the cocktail and the dessert. Look for complementary flavors and textures that will enhance each other. For example, a smoky and sweet cocktail may pair well with a dessert that is also sweet and smoky, such as a caramelized apple tart or a smoked chocolate cake.

Pair with the Occasion: Consider the occasion when pairing smoked cocktails with desserts. For a more casual event, such as a backyard barbecue, you may want to pair a smoky cocktail with a dessert that is more rustic, such as a smoked peach cobbler. For a more formal event, such as a dinner party, you may want to pair a smoky cocktail with a more elegant dessert, such as a smoked vanilla bean panna cotta.

Balance the Strength: When pairing smoked cocktails with desserts, it's important to balance the strength of both the cocktail and the dessert. A strong and bold cocktail may overpower a delicate dessert, while a mild cocktail may be overshadowed by a rich and flavorful dessert. For example, a smoky and bold cocktail may pair well with a chocolate lava cake, while a lighter and more delicate cocktail may pair well with a fruit tart.

Contrast the Flavors: Contrasting flavors is an excellent way to pair smoked cocktails with desserts. It creates a more complex and interesting flavor experience. For example, a smoky and sweet cocktail may pair well with a tart and tangy dessert, such as a citrus cheesecake. The contrast between the sweet and smoky cocktail and the tangy and citrusy dessert can create a unique and enjoyable taste sensation.

Pairing Ideas:

- Smoky Old Fashioned paired with smoked chocolate cake
- Mezcal Margarita paired with caramelized apple tart
- Smoked Bloody Mary paired with smoked bacon s'mores
- Smoked Whiskey Sour paired with smoked vanilla bean panna cotta
- Smoky Negroni paired with smoked honeycomb and cheese plate
- Smoked Manhattan paired with smoked almond biscotti
- Smoked Martinez paired with smoked pear and gingerbread tart
- Smoky Spiced Rum paired with smoked pumpkin pie
- Smoked Gin and Tonic paired with smoked lemon tart
- Smoky Mezcal Mule paired with smoked peach cobbler.

CONCLUSION

The art of smoked cocktails is a fascinating and complex world of mixology that brings together the time-honored tradition of smoking with the modern techniques of cocktail making. It is a blend of science and art, where every element - from the type of wood to the smoking technique, from the flavor profile to the glassware and garnish - plays a crucial role in creating a unique and memorable drinking experience.

We have explored the rich history of smoked cocktails, the different regional variations and classic recipes, as well as the modern interpretations and new techniques that have evolved over time. We have also delved into the chemistry of smoke and alcohol, the impact of wood on flavor and aroma, and the ways in which smoking can be used to create innovative and delicious drinks.

But the true joy of smoked cocktails lies in the endless possibilities for experimentation and creativity. Whether you are a professional mixologist or a home bartender, there is always room to push the boundaries and explore new flavor combinations. By understanding the various smoking techniques and their effects, and by considering the flavors and textures of different ingredients, you can create your own unique and flavorful cocktails that will leave a lasting impression on your guests. As with any form of mixology, safety is of the utmost importance when it comes to smoking cocktails. Proper ventilation, equipment handling, and fire safety precautions should always be followed to ensure a safe and enjoyable experience.

So, whether you prefer the classic smoky flavors of a Whiskey Sour or the modern twist of a Mezcal Margarita, let the art of smoked cocktails be your guide to a world of creativity, experimentation, and innovation. Raise your glass and toast to the magic of smoke and spirits, and to the endless possibilities of mixology. Cheers!

BOOK 4
TIKI DRINKS

INTRODUCTION

Tiki culture for decades has marked much of the mixing of the 900', introducing drinks with exotic flavors that manage to make you imagine the islands of the South Pacific. Tiki drinks are interesting and delicious taste experiences. But let's learn more about Tiki history and culture together.

The word Tiki is derived from Polynesian. Tiki culture was a phenomenon that influenced the entire United States in the 1930s through the 1970s. In those years there was a boom of Polynesian-themed clubs and restaurants, decorated with jungles and artificial elements. The spread of Tiki cocktails was born immediately after the period of Prohibition and the Great Depression, with the opening in 1931 of Don the Beachcomber, the first Polynesian-themed bar-restaurant in Hollywood by Ernest Raymond Beaumont Gantt, considered the father of tiki culture. To its diffusion in the second postwar period, together with Donn, gave a strong impulse also to the premises of Trader Vic (Victor J. Bergeron), another great exponent of the movement. The two were the authors of many cocktails, of which the most legendary are the Zombie (by Donn Beach) and the Mai Tai (by Trader Vic). The fortune of tiki, after more than 25 years of boom, began to decline in the seventies, to come back to the forefront from the first years of the new century.

Tiki cocktails are based on different types of rum mixed together with fruits, syrups, spices and infusions. Most tiki cocktails include at least one rum, although many combine up to three different types of sweet liquor. In true tropical style, Tiki drinks include fruit juices such as pineapple, orange, passion fruit, guava and coconut. The flavor is often dominated by the fruit, which often covers that of the alcohol. These drinks are anything but simple. The Tiki cocktail will often have four or more ingredients that create great depth in the flavor of the drink. Although not a requirement in a Tiki cocktail, many include spices, such as nutmeg, can be found in a number of Tiki recipes. There are many variations of Tiki coktails: the most famous are the Mai Tai, invented by Trader Vic, the Scorpion, the Zombie from Donn Beach and Don's Special Daiquiri. Tiki cocktails are usually served in classic ceramic glasses having the shape of humanoid faces or bodies: Tikis in Polynesian culture were representations of gods made on rocks or wood, having a great spiritual power.

In this book we will discover everything about this particular family of drinks: from the characterizing elements, to the typical liquors and the best recipes to test your skills. Are you ready to embark on this journey?

Have a good read,

pen name

MYSTERIES OF AN ANCIENT CIVILIZATION

No one knows the reason why about 2500 years ago from Southeast Asia strange and mythical double hulled sails moved towards the direction of the sun birth. But it is from that time that the history of the Tiki was born and in this chapter I will try to explain the meaning of the Tiki. No one yet knows why this migration took place, perhaps due to a natural disaster, to escape wars, persecution or for religious reasons. The fact is that these men sailed beyond the coasts and beyond the ocean, landing with families, supplies and animals in the warm oceanic islands.

The colonization of these uninhabited islands took place throughout the seas of Polynesia, Micronesia and Melanesia. By means of canoes, these populations crossed the bad weather of the seas and gradually pushed eastward, until they settled on the most distant islands, such as Easter Island.

BIRTH OF NEW POPULATIONS

After the settlement, these populations developed singular cultures that were similar to each other but at the same time different. Thus, in their customs and representative art, and therefore in their beliefs, they created isolated micro cultures protected by the natural environments of the small archipelagos. Micro cultures that have always been hidden from European civilization and the whole world, handed down from generation to generation, from father to son, almost confidentially, as if they were secrets. Secrets still today, considered mysteries. Today oceanic art is catalogued according to the different styles, or significant attitudes, that developed in the different areas.

COLONIZATION

We have known these cultures since the 1500s, when the first explorers, Spanish and Portuguese, by chance or by mistake, landed on these remote islands. The meager resources that these volcanic islands possessed gave way to attention to the natural surroundings in which they were immersed. Finding neither gold nor spices, the first visitors filled their logbooks with descriptions of the enchanting seas and skies with constellations never before seen. Over the centuries, the Spanish were succeeded by all the major European powers. Driven by the search for new gold resources and riches, they sought what the old known world could no longer guarantee. It is always thanks to the explorations that we know the physiognomy and part of the traditions of these populations. They were so different that they deserved in-depth studies and descriptions such as those reported by the legendary British captain.

TRIBAL PEOPLES

Populations of cannibals, heretics, unbelievers, violent headhunters and shameless naked women. In the sight of European missionaries, they were nothing more than primitive populations that needed to be converted. The deaths due to forced conversions decimated the populations. But not only, the contact with these isolated worlds favored the contamination of a fragile and different ecosystem that had remained unaltered until then. Not only that, unknown diseases and pathologies brought the native populations almost to extinction.

From the beginning, the first contacts with these new cultures were warlike and it didn't take long to enter in conflict with these men with primitive habits. Territoriality and defense of their villages was an innate characteristic for the natives. Accustomed to always defending their islands from surrounding tribes, their society formed warriors and headhunters.

Unequal battles, in favor of the Europeans, from galleys full of cannons it was not difficult to counter the territorial defense of the primitive populations. Of these warriors who poured into the sea with their canoes and armed with their primitive instruments of war. For these reasons most of the traditions and their beliefs, therefore of their culture, still remains a mystery. As it is still the meaning of their most ancient iconic representations. But we will see later that the most violent vicissitudes will soon be forgotten to make room for the beauty of these exotic paradises. Paradises that will be of inspiration to artists all over the world.

TIKI ART AND HISTORY

We know by now that every population distinguished itself in figurative art from archipelago to archipelago. Also from island to island therefore, the spirituality of their mystical divinities differed different humanoid artifacts with particular names and meanings.

Of all these artifacts very little has been deliberately destroyed by Europeans. So the precise meaning of what today is called oceanic art has been lost, an art that will remain forever steeped in fascinating doubts and mysteries. The English missionaries of the 1700's, intent on spreading their religion, burned all the ancient artifacts imprinted in the canoes and in what today we simply call Tiki. These mystical representations were part of the daily life of the natives and were not only part of the spiritual ceremonies. The spirituality of these expressions accompanied, fishing, hunting, as well as social occasions or war, up to funeral rituals.

MARQUESAS ISLANDS & MEANING OF TIKI

The history of the Tiki also derives from this culture and especially from the traditions that develop in the Marquesas Islands.

Meaning of the Tiki. A form of expression depicting "the image of something" and the personification of spirits represented on powerful humanoid carvings of stone, wood and human bone. In particular it is a tradition exclusive to the Marquesas Islands. Used to accompany and support mortuary rites, cannibalism, fishing, agriculture or magical healings and spiritual guarantees of fertility, the Tiki, like other representations of oceanic art, are not simply artistic representations. We can define them as eschatological concepts and attempts to explain, or at least justify, existence itself and all that was inexplicable. So the meaning of tiki is not 'referable to a single deity' as is often written!

The question arises spontaneously, *how is it possible and in what way we find again after two thousand five hundred years these representations in one of the most important and long-lived periods of the history of mixing? As the history of tiki, the meaning of Tiki of the Marquesas Islands is transformed into exotic culture?* Let's find out in the next chapter!

THE TIKI CULTURE

In the course of the history the Tiki Culture has assumed characters very different and divergent from the originality of the primitive and spiritual meaning. The word Tiki is today a container of concepts and arguments that invest an entire culture that has actually created a way of life that from America has involved the whole world. Precisely for this reason we speak of Tiki Culture. Tiki means mixing, but also music, cooking, entertainment and dance. Figurative arts that are graphics, paintings, sculptures, engravings, cinema. Tiki mugs and Hawaiian shirts. Areas of emotional and cultural involvement so diverse and disparate that Tiki Culture will even become a way of life, a way of thinking and a way of being.

THE SUCCESS OF THE TIKI CULTURE

Tiki is evasion, emotion. Tiki Culture was born as a means of escape from the dark times that America was going through because of the world wars. Being able to believe in the light-heartedness of living in an exotic and tropical dream was the only detachment from the reality of the time, and this is what Don the Beachcomber are able to make tangible. Tiki bars are the "forbidden island" where Americans drown their unattainable tropical dreams with huge quantities of rum. Donn Beach's cocktails are the means to live carefree social moments, so engaging that they will overwhelm the American culture to expand to the most popular tourist destinations. Over time, the expansion of this concept will bring everything related to the exotic, but also the tropical, to this single word. A container in which will be identified and incorporated, even in a completely wrong way, cultures and traditions that have nothing to do with the ancient primordial Tiki.

EXPANDING TIKI CULTURE

One of the most common examples is the mixing of this culture with ancient Hawaiian traditions. The most primitive and local customs will be mixed with an undefined and fake "Tiki tradition". The commodification of Hawaiian tradition will also lead to the complete destruction of native customs. The implementation of what economists refer to as "exotic imperialism" will bring effective American control of many tropical nations. Of this overpowering power enters fully the economic induced that the Tiki culture produces. Even the alcoholic tradition, which has always been a source of big business for the United States, is involved in this process of economic and therefore political control.

Gone are those ways of drinking that can actually be called tropical, born from the intertwining of European and African alcoholic cultures. Widespread in correlation to the increasing agricultural expansion and in particular to the cultivation of sugarcane are traditions of Caribbean islands. Unique products such as the ancient Hawaiian distillate Okolehao, will completely disappear in order to make room for dilapidated Tiki bottles actually containing bourbon.

As for mixing, one example out of all will be one of the most known cocktails in the world as Pina Colada in Cuba. Still today this cocktail is strictly connected to Tiki culture but in reality it has never had a concrete relation to Exotic or Tiki mixing, not even by accident. Contrary to what you will find written on the internet very often: *Pina Colada Is Not A Tiki Cocktail!*

Although it is incorporated into the exotic expansion of tiki culture, an umbrella on the drink is not enough to define a tiki cocktail or an exotic cocktail! But that's also why precisely the Tiki remains a social involvement that today would be called viral and, at the time, unprecedented. A phenomenon studied by sociologists and so influential in society to become a trend. A fashion that not only goes beyond the most primordial meanings, but is so different that it becomes a unique movement. The tiki culture will be a fashion will characterize in a predominant way forty years of the American 900'.

Becoming a real fashion, the movement will end up becoming completely anarchic with excessive and inconsiderate use of the themes of that Tiki culture invented by Donn Beach. With time the Tiki culture will not only lack originality but also a context, an outline, a structure and a content that in the past made it flourish. This is one of the reasons, in concomitance with other parallel social events, that will decree a wider and wider decline that culminates with the total collapse after the end of the 70's.

THE DECLINE OF TIKI CULTURE

But as specified at the beginning, the American vision of the exotic and of Tiki Culture has not always been uncontrolled and anarchic. As absurd as it may seem, all the arts mentioned up to now just mentioned are born from the mixing, from Don the Beachcomber's cocktail.

A mixing that instead, like the context created around it, will be extremely focused and studied, technical and difficult. The balance is inextricably linked to the study of products and ingredients in function of the exaltation of the distillate. Donn Beach and "his greatest imitators" teach us that through contextualized mixing it is possible to create not only interest, but involvement and emotion.

We will discover that the techniques that Donn Beach puts into practice for the exaltation of the distillate in new exotic flavors are still concretely relevant today. Thanks to them, we will discover that the Tiki Culture, being an idea, a concept, a way of being and living, is never dead. It lives and it is still stronger than the mere nostalgic feeling for past times.

DIFFERENCE BETWEEN TIKI AND TROPICAL

I believe that the confusion stems from a wrong approach that often affects Tiki, both from the point of view of mixing and in its social involvement. A plausible confusion, as neither of the two blends belongs to our culture. But it is also evident that sometimes those who try to divulge it do not do it in the right way. Juxtaposing Tiki and Tropical is wrong! Let's try together to understand why.

1st Reason: Tiki Bars

There is no doubt that, since its birth, the Tiki is evocative of vacation atmospheres, carefree inserted in the reproduction of a basically tropical climate. Tropical plants, flowers and evocations of Polynesian and Caribbean traditions are the background of the very first Tiki Bars and Luau, the Tiki theme parties. However this is an environment far from the real tropical or Polynesian life, distorted, which does not respect in any way the tropical culture. But this is not the end of the story because, very soon, the Tiki breaks away from this tropical vision and takes on an identity of its own, detaching itself more and more from the tropical one! This style is the Exotic Pop.

Exotic pop is detached from tropical in form and content. So different that it is even exported to those tropical places where, ideally, it should have existed naturally. We can conclude by saying that the setting and the tropical themes of the Tiki Bars must not be confused with the mixing practiced by the bartenders of the time. Donn Beach, who created the Tiki, his imitators, followers and successors, in all the fifty evolutionary years of the Tiki, have never served tropical cocktails in Tiki Bars!

2nd Reason: Tropical Fruit & Rum

Today we tend to see Tiki as a fruit-rich mix, perhaps tropical fruit, but that is not the case. Donn Beach used to buy hundreds of coconuts from Hawaii and yet none of his Tiki drinks have coconut in them. He bought pineapple and passion fruit, but he didn't serve Pina Colada or Batide. Pineapple was not included in small doses in his drinks until twenty years after his exotic style was born. Passion fruit was never used fresh, but only after being processed. Rather, Tiki is a RUM-rich mix! And we tell you more, only certain types of rum.

Donn was the foremost expert on rums, blending and Caribbean culture so he carefully selected traditional rum characteristics to blend into his exotic drinks, but not all rums were suitable for his blending. He didn't make Tiki drinks with herbaceous, acidic, young rums. He didn't make anything like a T-punch or a Caipirinha. He never crushed limes or fresh fruit, and he didn't use spiced rum or arrangè rum. He didn't mix tropical cocktails.

3rd Reason: Tropical Influences On Tiki

What do ancient punches have to do with Tiki? Technically nothing. The Tiki drink stems from the most advanced technique of tropical cocktails, that of Constante's Daiquiri. In Donn's Tiki Bar, an American mix is served suitable for the American palate and for Americans who wanted to drink exotic from Florida to Alaska.

Donn was so knowledgeable and aware of tropical drinking and traditions that he doesn't even replicate them; he knows it's not suited to the American palate. The same Americans who, heedless of tropical culture, gorged themselves on whiskey and beer at Sloppy Joe's. For those who do not know, Sloppy Joe's is one of the most famous bars in Cuba. We can say that the Tiki mixing was born taking inspiration from a mixing style already defined, and probably the most advanced of the time, that of Constantino Ribalaigua, the brilliant bartender who revolutionized the Daiquiri, which in turn Donn evolved into the most difficult mixing of all time.

Warning. You don't have to see the Tiki drink as an evolution of Cuban mixing which, in turn, had already been influenced by traditional American mixing. The Tiki is a new mixing concept that takes its cue from certain techniques and ingredients and evolves into exotic mixing not in Cuba but, as we know, in California. Today the Tiki is a container in which are inserted many similar mixing styles. However they all belong to the same American cultural and social period. We can call Tikis Exotic Cocktails but not Tropical Cocktails!

At this point we are left with only one possible question...What is Tropical Mixing?

We have understood that Tiki is an elaborated mixing because it has been studied and conceived at the table, not by chance, the same cannot be said about Tropical mixing. Tropical is pure tradition. It is an ancient tradition, far from the bar and the Tiki Bar, which dates back to the dawn of the birth of today's Caribbean populations and then spread in part of South America. It is the union of ancient cultures that has favored exchanges of traditions coming from every part of the world. The same knowledge which also made possible the birth and development of the Caribbean distillate par excellence, rum. But the tropical is not only sugar cane, but also fermented and distilled, native ways of drinking lost time.

They are the memory of the most ancient African and European alcoholic traditions which were born from the fruits of the earth. Preparations that, starting from the 1500s, trigger an evolutionary process that goes back more than four hundred years before Tiki. For this reason we still do not understand how these 400 years of history can be united in a "Tiki and Tropical. The difference between Tiki and Tropical is clear.

Donn Beach's Tiki was created to exalt and bring out the qualities of a distillate which is more and more sought-after, whereas Tropical drinking was created to mask and hide the faults of a primordial distillate. Tiki and Tropicale cannot be compared to each other. Tiki and Tropicale are blends which differ in the products, in the drinks, in the technique and in a drastic way in the culture in which they evolve.

Tropical mixing is born from a way of drinking which is not technical but raw like the ancient self produced spirits, undefined, aguardiente and early rum. Far from the products of Tiki Bars. Rough like the vicissitudes of the populations that created it: distillates, punch and then cocktails that over the centuries became immortal symbols of the pride of subjugated cultures.

Between myths and legends this way of drinking becomes a real modern mixing! Stories of pirates, sailors, rebels, farmers, corsairs, workers, slaves and cimarrones, are shaped to form the most popular tropical cocktails today, between customs and rituals.

Tropical is a mixing with few certainties. Just think that even today there are questions about the actual origin of the word rum. And it is necessary to unravel four hundred years of sources in order to understand how a pressed pineapple becomes a Piña Colada. As it happens for many tropical cocktails. There are no cookbooks or bartenders' books that can attest to this centuries-old culture.

The stories of the first travelers, diaries, descriptions or notes of some more or less famous writer lead us to understand how a tradition, a cocktail, was born from a necessary way of drinking. On the contrary, Donn's Tiki is an always identifiable cocktail, as it is born from a pondered study. The tropical drink, unlike Tiki drinks, is not born defined, but it is simply an autochthonous way of drinking, absolutely traditional and variable as the Italian "ragù della nonna" that in time has evolved and is still evolving.

In conclusion: tiki drink is part of a mixing studied for an American palate, rich in aged rums, to which are also added traditional European liquors, such as anise or orange liqueurs. As opposed to the tropical one, in tiki is tried to exalt the distillate and tropical fruits such as pineapple are not present. Tropical is instead a tradition which evolves during centuries and becomes what we know today: drinks having a simple structure, rich in young and raw distillates and fresh fruit. Simple drinks but not banal, so much that drinking a good Piña Colada or a good Mojito is very difficult. Everyone thinks they know how to prepare them correctly, but it is evident to everyone that it is not so.

TIKI MIXING: VARIATIONS BETWEEN ERAS

Defining Tiki mixing by outlining single and peculiar characteristics of ingredients, techniques and styles is undoubtedly limiting and reductive. In this chapter I will try to explain how drinks which are now defined as Tiki can actually be cocktails having diametrically opposed characteristics and yet they can belong to this great category which is generally defined as Tiki only. I will analyze why Donn's drinks are different from those of Trader Vic as well as from those of Filipino mixologists and we will see how even great classics can actually become Tiki drinks.

WHAT IS MEANT BY TIKI MIXING?

We can surely say that the word Tiki, intended as Tiki mixing, is the longest time reference when compared to other trendy or fashionable mixing paths in the history of mixing itself. From the period of activity of the man who is considered the originator of mixed drinking, Jerry Thomas, mixing has a history of about two hundred years of life of which about fifty to sixty years have been incredibly influenced by Tiki.

The Tiki mixing is born and changes in relation to the time, to the variation of the economic curve, of the social state, therefore of the political, military and imperialist influences of the country, it changes then also in line with the development of the culture, of the technology and of the tourism therefore it changes to the change of the habits of the Americans. The Tiki mixing incorporates the past and present history to become, after its end, an integral part of the history of the United States and therefore in turn influential of subsequent periods. So for this reason, at the beginning of the Tiki Era, in an atmosphere with a background of Exotica music born from the ashes of the roaring Jazz Age we can see Fred Astaire or Frank Sinatra drinking a Navy Grog at the counter of Donn Beach and rediscover the powerful intensity of an old fashioned. On the opposite side instead, the aftermath of an era now dead, we can see Eminem, in 1995 at the Chin Tiki in Detroit, drinking a fresh, long and light drink of dubious quality served in a Tiki mug with the background and words of an old school rap song.

For these reasons, today we talk about Tiki Era, Polynesian Pop and Tiki Culture. Fifty years are obviously nothing if compared to our millenary culture and to our historical periods, but they become extremely important if we consider that the history of the United States can be counted in a few hundred years.

Tiki mixing is therefore a great container of different styles and flavors that vary in time but always and exclusively contextualized to the historical period. The different techniques are born and change in time always in order to reach the goal of this contextualization representing the society in the present time and they are supported only by the quality of the final product. For this reason today it is not enough to change an ingredient to create a twist of a Tiki cocktail but it is necessary to evaluate the concept and the contextualization of the period in order to relate it to today.

THE BIRTH OF TIKI// THE FIRST ERA

It is undoubtedly correct to say that all this history was born exclusively thanks to Tiki mixing or, as I prefer to say, thanks to the exotic cocktail of Donn Beach, without which Tiki culture could not have existed. Thanks to Donn's technique he is able to express unique and never known flavors, so original as to be credible as a tangible proof of the existence of a fake exotic paradise in which people believe, bewitched by the taste of the exotic cocktail.

Donn creates a cocktail for a people with a strong alcoholic tradition and at the same time for a static society depressed by wars, social and economic crises, that sitting at the bar was used to drown in alcohol pains, dissatisfaction and zero prospects. Through the technique of Constante Donn creates a new way to conceive cocktails with aged rum as no one has ever done before, he works the pure ingredient in order to make it express instantly in its most closed and hidden scents and combining various rums he manages to create unique and original aromas.

As a matter of fact Donn's drinks are technically Daiquiris but they have nothing to do with the freshness and drinkability of a Daiquiri. Donn's drinks are static, still and powerful, almost for meditation, they do not evolve in time but they remain the same for the whole duration of the drink. They are drunk slowly immersed in an environment that, correlated to these new scents, transports the customer literally for hours and hours in another world.

The American at Donn's time was surely a heavy drinker just out of prohibitionism, therefore besides having a great thirst he felt the need and the desire to detach himself from a mentally and economically oppressive period. The only way to do this was to fantasize and transport his mind elsewhere. Donn's drinks were therefore pure concentrate of aromas and power, very small in size, practically even though they had different shapes they were not much bigger than a cocktail glass. For the same reason the Tiki mixing of the Tiki Era in which Donn lived was static, every sip had to express the same explosion from the beginning to the end. Although the alcoholic amount was generally much larger than today's standards, the modern customer would probably be disappointed by the small size of the tumbler served at Don The Beachcomber.

The explosion of which I speak is only achieved with great mastery of the raw material, namely rums, which worked only exclusively with the milkshake mixer and with the correct use of ice give unique and original flavors. There is no other way to replicate Donn's mixing.

This and only this technique allows to mix quantities of alcohol that no other technique can balance. The alcoholic charge is largely outclassed by the texture created by the technique and by the aromatic explosion of the ingredients. The exact degree of dilution, which does not change in time, makes the drink always the same. Thanks to this technique it is possible to make unapproachable drinks such as Zombie (later on in the book we will learn how to make it).

To say it is an ancient technique and not very replicable today is absurd, indeed I would say the opposite, even though the rums used by Donn do not exist anymore, applying this technique to modern mixing, with the quantity and quality of today's products would give new life to all the sixty drinks Donn had on his menu. As I always say there are no rums for tasting and rums for mixing, all rums are also for mixing, indeed the more the rum is qualitative the more the drink is good.

Moreover, many of the expensive distillates studied for the market of smooth consumption, but of low quality, compromise the quality of the drink when mixed, in particular those with various congeners and too many added sugars. Personally, in order to distinguish this category of Tiki cocktails by Donn, I prefer to call them exotic cocktails, not only because at that time the word Tiki did not define mixing yet, but also because, as we will see, they are clearly distinguished from those of its successors.

EVOLUTION OF COCKTAILS// THE SECOND ERA

As already mentioned what differentiates styles in tiki mixing is the contextualization to society and it would be absurd to think about a static society. After the first years of Donn's mixing, precisely after the second world war, the sense of revenge of Americans is pushed by a growing economic wellness which involves the whole nation, a wellness which gives the possibility to move and to move, tourism was born.

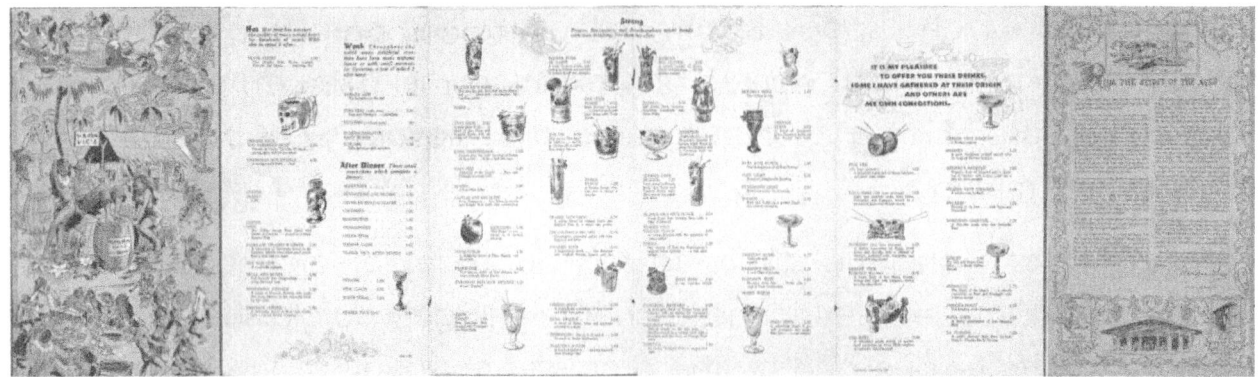

This desire for lightness and light-heartedness is understood and perceived in advance by Trader Vic who, through his technique, manages to create a Tiki mix that is easily combined with an increasingly fast and dynamic society.

Just as Donn understood the needs of society by expressing them in his cocktails, Vic does exactly the same thing by creating light and carefree drinks. Different cocktails, opposite to those of Donn and yet born from the same matrix. It is not by chance that the Mai Tai, born in that structure in the 40's, in the middle of the "Donn era", will be successful only from the middle of the 50's.

Yet even by analyzing his most famous drink, the Mai Tai, as well as all the other previous and following drinks it is evident that he derived a masterful interpretation of Daiquiri. Even for Trader Vic's drinks it is demonstrable that they are Constant Daiquiris. Vic studied in Cuba and evolved by interpreting Donn Beach. This does not make him a mere imitator but an innovator, as Donn was in his time. Once again the sacred triad of Caribbean mixing is twisted on a technical level to give a purpose to the drink that is still different but contextualized to a new society.

Trader Vic's drinks are fresh, light, simple and aromatic, not only rum but many distillates, they are also very simple and fast to make. Very important is that they are easily recognizable in order to be remembered by customers. Although simple they are anything but banal.

Distillates are almost always acolics with less pretension, less full bodied, less aromatic, less structured, they do not have a great need to open up but they must immediately grant instant aromatic power and support the balance of the whole cocktail with a good shoulder of alcohol.

Distillates such as gin london dry (crisp and dry) or bourbon (warm and smooth), or Cuban rum (liqueur) do not need a great evolution in order to release different aromas from the impact of the first esters and they are far from the complexity of the great aged Demerara or Jamaica rums used by Donn.

Their exaltation takes place by adding a strong acidity which sometimes is exaggerated but after few sips it enlarges the aromatic palette of the drink. Initially the drink can seem to be difficult to drink but the palate rapidly gets used to the acidity and is able to perceive a very intense aromatic explosion in a short time, despite the drink is light and extremely fresh. These drinks in fact, are studied to be drunk in large numbers, in a fast and non stationary way, maybe on the beach in Hawaii, in a bar, in a kiosk, in a swimming pool and then again in another bar by tourists wearing Hawaiian shirts. A Trader Vic's drink with two ounces of alcohol seems non-alcoholic.

Generally these drinks, as opposed to Donn drinks, because of their structure, would evolve in time and would become bad, watered down and inconsistent, especially because their function as a thirst quencher makes them bigger and bigger and therefore more and more showy. However in reality this problem does not arise because they are studied to be drunk in a rapid and continuous way and therefore the sense is to finish them before a change of state. A fast and dynamic drinking in "Cuban Daiquiri" style, which in fact has only a Cuban name, but reflects the way of life of those who in American Cuba drank Daiquiri.

PARALLEL TIKI MIXING

So far I have described the two most important macro categories in the history of Tiki mixing. From these styles will emerge numerous bartenders and cocktails sometimes even superior to those of Donn Beach or Trader Vic.

During the first era Donn's secrets were mostly mimicked and reinterpreted by everyone on the wave of success which was becoming fashionable. The many bars that were born soon after often just took advantage of the success of Donn's cocktail names by reproducing shapes and colors. But the luckiest ones could boast the support of bartenders with a training that came from Donn's own employees.

In time, the Filipinos who left Don the Beachcomber landed as protagonists in the best Tiki bars of America, directly training their successors with the techniques and secrets they were able to guess from Donn. This very particular style, I still don't know how much intentionally, has become a unique characteristic of Filipino bartenders descending from Donn. Probably a style born unconsciously from the lack of propensity for creativity but also thanks to their great talent as performers.

The Filipino Tiki bartending community is closely tied to Donn's story. Back in Los Angeles with his forward thinking ideas but with no money left Don was helped by many Filipinos as he worked to support himself.

Among the many jobs he held in parking lots, car washes and the fruit market Don promised these people that one day, once he had his own business, he would hire them all. So he did, particularly with the first four Filipino mixologists.

Filipinos who were excellent performers, fast and with great gifts for service did indeed become good at it. But in spite of the technical evolution of the tools and the new style brought by Trader Vic, Filipinos, once they started their independent career as bartenders, kept, maybe simply out of habit, the use of the technical style learned by Donn.

However Donn's technique will be applied also to recipes with softer ingredients, making drinks lighter than the difficult and intense Tiki mixing of the 30's. Parallel to Vic's mixing, around the 50's was born a different Tiki mixing. In this case rum is still the protagonist but in a different context because a mixing as powerful as Donn's obviously could not be adapted to modern society.

However excellent drinks were created such as Big Bamboo, Puka Punch, or many others of classic inspiration such as Black Magic or Doctor Wong. The addition of soft ingredients, therefore a greater use of fresh juices (citric in particular) and syrups is not implemented as in the big Trader Vic's drinks, (e.g. fog cutter, potted parrot, scorpion etc.) but is concentrated in small glasses with Donn's technique.

This gave origin to very intense cocktails but at the same time fresh cocktails in which, thanks to the technique, also the aromas of non-alcoholic elements are exalted in an exponential way. It goes without saying that in order to obtain the best results ingredients must be fresh and excellent.

THE CONTAMINATION OF CLASSICS WITH TIKI MIXING

If Filipinos take back very faithfully Donn's mixing and redevelop it for their time, we can often find very classic cocktail structures subjected to Tiki mixing. Excluding in fact the technical categories described above, it happens to find among tiki drinks some drinks such as julep, old fashioned, sour, hot punch and so on.

As said at the beginning, Tiki is a big container that embraces history and creates history, therefore it also includes past cultures of mixing and therefore also the traditional ways of drinking and the common use of Americans. So even the great classics if well contextualized can enter and become part of the Tiki concept. To justify these contaminations with an example.

Can an old fashioned be a Tiki cocktail? My answer is yes, if contextualized in the right way. The Old Fashioned is a way of drinking a distillate, presumably created to improve it as all the ways of drinking of the ancient traditions, today, for pleasure, we drink and prepare it instead with the intent to enhance that distillate. What if you wanted to drink the legendary rum blend of the Mai Tai or a Navy Grog in a different way?

Even Mai Tai is to all intents and purposes a way of drinking rum, a drink that has a reason to exist because of the concept it represents but which is able to express itself thanks to the famous blend of rums that made history. If a rum lover would like to drink the blend of rums that make up Mai Tai with the same balance but with a different expressive technique he or she could do it by creating an old fashioned ad hoc.

Sure, it is undoubtedly another drink but for this reason, even though Mai Tai Old Fashioned or Navy Grog, are different drinks from the traditional ones they keep some key concepts which are however part of the original tiki drinks. The characteristics of those rum blends with another technique will obviously give different expressions.

Donn himself sometimes used classic techniques to express some particularities of rums. To make another example 151 Swizzle, which is undoubtedly a Donn's drink, however it can be considered as a Tiki is in fact a Julep, therefore contextualized in the right way even a julep can be a Tiki drink. Probably the only way to be able to drink in purity and appreciate the characteristics of a 151 proof. Hot punches, coffee grogs and hot buttered are also of primary importance for Tiki mixing of all times and yet they are much older ways of drinking even than the cocktail itself. These, which today are categories of drinks, are the most ancient ways of drinking in the history of spirits but by becoming traditional in the centuries they also undergo the influence of Tiki. They are therefore contextualized to the period and embellished with exotic flavors thanks to home made, spices and non traditional ingredients.

Kona Coffee Grog, for example, is one of Donn's most famous drinks as well as Trader Vic's Hot Butter Rum Batter.

In fact, tiki mixing, in all its forms, teaches us different techniques and makes us understand how much the bar reflects society as a place of involvement and expression.

The bar in fact, in all its forms, ancient and future, was and will always be the fulcrum of social aggregation that involves and manages to convey any extraction. Whether this expression has been artistic, revolutionary, literary, subversive or illicit it has always been accompanied by drinking manners that reflected the needs of people all over the world in any context. Basically the needs of man have always been the same and cyclically they appear in the years with different forms related to the present. Tiki mixing in particular teaches us that innovation, with reference to techniques, takes place by adapting and reworking them in order to allow the drink to express the needs, the way of living or the way of wanting to live that are perceived in a specific historical moment. For this reason many of the cocktails of the Tiki era are immortal and lapidary because they are representative of the history of the society itself.

TIKI MUG: JUST MARKETING?

Tiki Glasses and Tiki Mugs, what is the meaning of these items? Why are they so important for Tiki cocktails and Tiki bars. The biggest mistake we can make is to consider Tiki mugs only scenic, let's see why.

FROM THE FIRST EXOTIC TIKI BAR TO THE TIKI MUG

We have seen how exotic cocktails become part of American drinking habits when some drinks such as the Zombie leave the exclusive context of Tiki Bars and become part of the category of classic cocktails. Donn Beach's genius becomes tangible when he starts serving a new concept of Daiquiri. A drink particularly appreciated by Americans who had already learned about it when they frequented Cuba.

Beyond the technique and the mixing style I told how the astonishment of Don the Beachcomber's customers was triggered by the way he served his exotic potions. Weird glass beakers, often similar to those used for soda drinks that dispensed the countless American soda fountains, shells, hollowed out pineapples and coconuts. Repurposed containers, such as classic pilsner glasses, which in a short time begin to be cataloged just as Tiki glasses. Even the simple collins in which Zombie was served will soon be known and sold as Zombie glass.

THE FIRST TIKI GLASSES

Although Donn did not use the famous Tiki Mugs, which did not exist yet, every tiki glass, new or adapted, undoubtedly aroused great astonishment in the customer. A great visual and emotional impact considering that in the post prohibition period the glasses used by bars were practically only tumblers and cocktail cups. The bars, however, hosted a clientele largely unaccustomed to proper mixed drinks and that poured into the bars with the memory of the old American way of drinking called old fashioned, a concept not only limited to cocktails or type of glass service.

Donn applied a new type of service, accurate and studied in detail that, unlike what it may seem, was not only a function of image but had a very important technical purpose. In fact, we can notice that every single cocktail was always served in only one kind of glass, distinguishable, unique and with the right and precise size for that kind of drink.

An ingenious idea that, as I have already said, goes beyond suggestion because in this way Donn manages to facilitate the identification of the drink by the customer. A client who may not remember or know what is inside the drink but, through the image of the glass, can identify the flavor of a past experience. Especially considering a new and complex mixing like Donn's.

It is not by chance that many cocktails will give their name to the type of glass in which they were served, just like the old fashioned mentioned before. As already mentioned, very important is also the size of the glass, the elegant, precise and meticulous balance of Donn's drink does not allow any mistake and, for a perfect result, the quantity contained in the glass must always be the same. For this reason every cocktail had its own glass and it was almost always made of glass. We can therefore understand that the use of the Tiki Mug as we intend it today, for cocktails of Donn's first Tiki era, is not really suitable.

BIRTH AND DIFFUSION OF THE TIKI MUG

While Donn Beach exalted the clientele with the mysteries of his rum potions, the popularity of Don the Beachcomber seemed to have no boundaries and many competitors tried, unsuccessfully, to imitate him. The difficulty of this undertaking has increased the need to focus attention on the image of the drink rather than on techniques and unknown ingredients. Undoubtedly the secrecy Donn kept in preparing his potions did not help, therefore the first imitations were limited to replicate the colors of the drinks and the glasses in which they were served, while trying to increase the attention by exalting the image of the bars and the cocktails themselves.

Not being able to focus on the technical quality, the visual image of the drink was more and more amplified, sometimes even extreme. So it was that in the 50's somewhere in California, in one of the countless Tiki Bars, mysteriously appeared the first Tiki Mug. Which one, where, how and when is not known. There are many theories but few certainties. A concept, that of the Tiki cups, taken from the ancient oceanic culture. Culture we remember dating back more than two thousand years ago, when sculptures with humanoid shapes were carved to contain the spirits in order to take advantage through their power in earthly attitudes.

But that's not all, some Tiki glasses were produced taking inspiration from human skulls or symbols that ancient Headhunter warriors carried around as heirlooms to acquire greater spiritual strength. The Tiki object therefore, in its more spiritual and oceanic art meaning, goes from being a mystic and millenary eschatological symbol to a nice and terrifying artistic object of the XX century, used to contain cocktails.

Since the birth of the Tiki mug the fantasy in the reproduction of these spiritual entities in Tiki glasses is wasted and it will be this object that will bring the Tiki in its second era. In reality the Tiki Mug is one of those cases in which artistic expression is not an end in itself but becomes truly functional.

Imbued with the spirituality of every single expression, Tiki mugs become objects of worship and marketing, symbols of many Tiki bars and many Tiki cocktails. A contextualized cultural icon, an evocative, symbolic and decorative object, it is current and fun to think that in every Tiki Mug an ancient spirit is hidden. Often the mug is the identifying symbol not only of the cocktail but of the place itself, of which it bears the name or vice versa, and in which the most important drinks are served. In this regard it is impossible to forget the legendary Tiki Bob.

TRADER VIC AND THE TIKI MUGS

If even today we do not know who exactly invented the Tiki Mug or where it was first used, we can instead say with certainty that it is thanks to Trader Vic that these cups are the object of great diffusion. They became fashion and a true cult for collectors. Trader Vic made a great use of Tiki Mugs but, just like Donn did with his glasses, he contextualized them for each cocktail through original and identifying styles. And because of this, like Donn's cocktails, some of Vic's drinks have become immortal through the image expressed by the mug.

Not only that, each cup bearing the name of the Tiki cocktail of reference could be purchased in the shops of the clubs becoming souvenirs and collector's items. By spreading the name of the drink and of the club itself Trader Vic found a way to monetize from what was in fact also a publicity operation, in every part of the world there was someone who had some Trader Vic's branded cups at home. In the 60's, when tourism touches the top of its expansion, it was almost unthinkable to go to a Trader Vic's without coming home with a Tiki Mug.

Hawaii would be invaded by these strange mugs despite the fact that the word Tiki is not a prerogative of Hawaiian culture but of the Marquesas Islands. And so it was that tourists and travelers, from the most famous volcanic islands in the world, will bring mugs around the world. Even one of the oldest Hawaiian drinks, the Scorpion, became a Tiki cocktail served in the Scorpion bowl, again by the hand of Trader Vic.

ART AND FANTASY IN TIKI BARS

In general, the style of Tiki cups is not very consistent with ancient oceanic artistic expressions. As we have seen, the ancient figurative arts are similar but different in all the cultures that crept into the small oceanic archipelagos. So there are at the same time tiki cups shaped like Moai from Easter Island, headhunter, Tiki from the Marquesas Islands and Tiki cups of pure fantasy and style often designed by famous artists. But the cups that enter the history, at that time almost totally produced in Japan, will be only those that will be contextualized to precise Tiki cocktails.

It is not by chance that Trader Vic's are still today among the most sought after ones. Some mugs have brought drinks to an unthinkable success, just for the ease of identification and for the beauty and originality of the mug itself. In this regard, it is curious to imagine the expression of the legendary Joe Shalom, inventor of the first Suffering Bastard, when, arrived in the United States, customers who ordered a Suffering Bastard did not expect his drink but the drink and the mug invented by Trader Vic. Completely different cocktail to which he had given the same name.It is not by chance that Trader Vic's are still today among the most sought after ones. Some mugs have brought drinks to an unthinkable success, just for the ease of identification and for the beauty and originality of the mug itself.

In this regard, it is curious to imagine the expression of the legendary Joe Shalom, inventor of the first Suffering Bastard, when, arrived in the United States, customers who ordered a Suffering Bastard did not expect his drink but the drink and the mug invented by Trader Vic. Completely different cocktail to which he had given the same name. Some clubs have entered history and will never be forgotten for the symbolic and collectable value of their representative tiki glasses. For example, as already mentioned, the mythical Tiki Bob mug of the homonymous club designed by the artist Alec Yuill Thornton or the Mr. Bali Hai of the Bali Hai club.

The Tiki mug becomes a real and proper artistic object that attracts the attention of great artists who produce unique and very valuable artifacts. To cite two famous places it is the case of the mugs of Kahiki or those of Steve Crane's Luau, objects whose value of the artist is much higher than the material object itself.

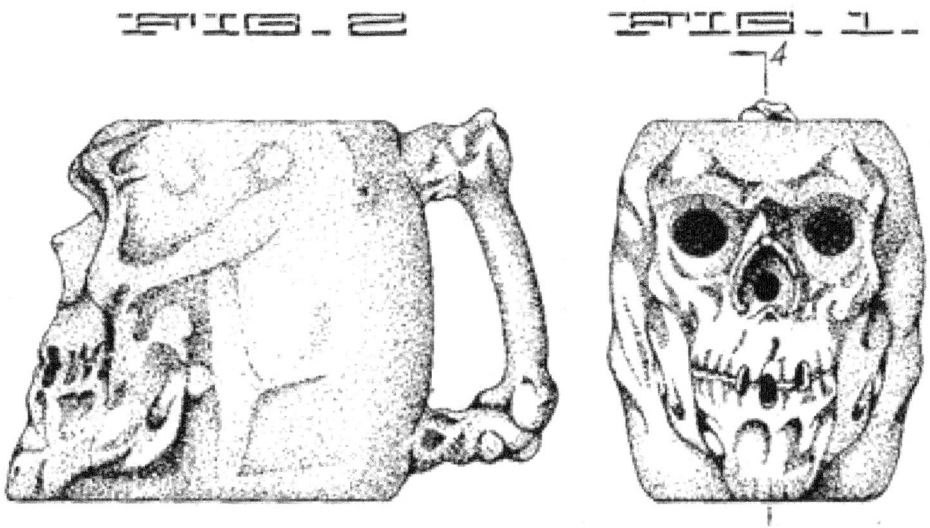

Even Trader Vic, an art lover, made many of the prototypes of tiki glasses used in his clubs, very famous as the double wall skulls for hot coffee grog. Even today the most modern mugs are collectors' items, even though they do not have a historical value or they are not specifically related to a bar or a cocktail, they are made by internationally renowned artists and for this reason they reach very high values. This is the case of Van Tiki's productions or the ones having designs by Shag, Bosko etc. Finally to be mentioned is also the wide use made by Walt Disney in the Trader

Sam's bar of his famous playground. Not only that, the company's passion for Tiki is so evident that often even other characters related to the famous brand have been reproposed as Tiki mugs.

HOW TO MAKE TIKI COCKTAIL TWISTS

The subject of Tiki cocktail twists is particularly dear to my heart. Often I have been criticized for being too conservative and traditionalist and therefore not very permissive to the "development" of this wide and complex mixing. In reality, I simply believe that the only way to replicate and possibly develop and innovate a technique is to know it fully and practice it.

But I am convinced that technique is not enough. The bar, the alcohol, therefore the mixing, has always been a manifest of the society, of its change, in the well-being and in the vicissitudes. The Tiki, from this point of view, is undoubtedly the mixing that most expresses the values and failures of the society of the time. It was born in order to express a need and in its decades it evolved similarly to society itself. *Simply put, it's not enough to throw down a couple of rum, passion fruit, pineapple and lime to make a tiki cocktail.*

Making tiki cocktail twists is not immediate and it is a broad concept to describe and one that you can hardly learn online, let alone on my blog, even if I were better than Donn Beach. Stories are told through the airwaves but no one became proficient in martial arts by watching Bruce Lee movies. Of course as always it takes study, observation, practice. A bartender with a good palate and good technique is a good bartender. A bartender with a good palate, a good technique and a good culture is a great bartender, because when he manages to express that culture, that concept in the cocktail, he acquires his own style. This is also true for cultures in reference to drinks from other eras regarding twists.

THE TWISTS OF TIKI COCKTAILS

In this chapter I will talk about the conceptual value of the Tiki cocktail, while in the next chapter I will focus more on the choice of ingredients and processing techniques. Actually, I have always thought that in making Tiki cocktail twists, one can use ALL ingredients. All ingredients that are appropriate to express the concept of the original cocktail and therefore properly processed in order to achieve the technical result to be expressed, regardless of the flavor. I will talk about this in the next chapter. In this chapter I will try to explain what is behind the Tiki cocktail beyond a technical research, of taste and beyond the ingredients themselves.

What do I mean by the original cocktail concept?

Tiki cocktails in general are the most difficult to replicate, not only because some, such as Donn's, are studied from the beginning with a high balancing difficulty, but because, they presuppose a basic historical/cultural knowledge from which they are born. Tiki cocktails are often born as concepts which are then expressed by balancing the multiplicity and diversity of rums. Twists in Tiki cocktails must necessarily keep in mind these concepts, once respected there are no limits to variations and therefore to the use of new products.

TRADITIONAL APPROACH

The premise to be made right away is that Tiki blending was born as an exclusive blending of RUMs and then developed over time with other distillates as well. In the section where I talk about the origin of Donn's mixing, it is clear that the innovation is purely derived from the TECHNICAL development of Constante's mixing, that of Daiquiri. But we cannot say that Donn's cocktails are twists of Constantino Ribalaigua's cocktails because the concept of the drinks is completely different, if it were not so we could not talk about innovation. And we should not be fooled by the tropical, exotic, Polynesian context in which these drinks were served. A flowered shirt is not enough to be able to serve or twist tiki cocktails.

These exotic contents of decoration represent rather the idealization of a dream, the need to detach the mind from reality, from a social climate at the time repressive, gray and inadequate. The actualization of this idea, therefore the dreamlike atmosphere of exotic bars, became extremely real only thanks to the involvement of all human sensory capacities, none excluded. To accentuate these feelings in fact the first bars were closed environments, without windows or glimpses of the life of society outside the bar, a total detachment to immerse themselves and live fully the atmosphere.

Today there is probably no need or even feasibility for such a binding physical location to drive customers and everyone would be more focused on the phone anyway. So Tiki and Twist Tiki cocktails can be drunk anywhere. But in recreating a Tiki bar, it is the same if we think of the current fashion of speakeasies, the bar should be reinterpreted with a certain criterion and relevance to the original concept of the time. A neon sign with the writing Tiki is not Tiki, wallpaper with tropical plants from Ikea is not Tiki. The same goes for cocktails. The exotic settings of these places, so far from "normality", so "strange" and surreal, became concrete and made sense in their form only thanks to the tangibility of the cocktail invented by Donn. It was never important to know if this fiction, tending to replicate the Polynesian atmosphere, was actually representative of and faithful to the real climate of those distant and mysterious places. It was only important that it was real there, in the bar, at that moment. It became real and tangible in that precise moment in which, thanks to the cocktail, it took on its own identifying flavor. This precise and new flavor, evocative of memories, emotions, desires, sensations, is the only reason why these drinks, in particular the drinks of Donn Beach have become immortal. So powerful that they are also able to evoke memories never experienced, to make you dream.

THE CONCEPTUAL VALUE OF TIKI

It is axiomatic to say that over 50 years of history would not have existed without the exotic cocktail, therefore that the Tiki era would not have existed without Don the Beachcomber. It is therefore unthinkable to believe that the longevity of Tiki is only due to the particular goodness of cocktails, this is therefore a heavy heritage to be expressed by replicating or trying to make twist of Tiki cocktails. Undoubtedly then, the conceptual value of the cocktail, starting from the name, must necessarily be taken into consideration when making twists of Tiki cocktails of the time, but also when making a new drink.

As an example, many of Donn's drinks bore names referring to the war or to the military world, not by chance, not only for the direct experiences that Donn lived but, in a post-war period, obviously it was a theme that tied and accumulated a great part of the American society, and ignited the call of the oceanic islands glimpsed and narrated by veterans.

This conceptual value of the cocktail is more important than the recipe itself and is expressed in its highest meaning, even stronger and more engaging, about 25 years after Donn's mixing, by Trader Vic's Mai Tai.

The Mai Tai, even though it is representative of the expression of a different society from the one in which Donn mixed, in some ways opposite, in every reinterpretation of it, in relation to the ingredients, has always been a twist of a drink that no one has ever really known, with products and rums that practically never even existed in bars or at least unknown to most people.

The conceptual expression of the cocktail is immortalized by the rum and the individual blends of the rums are in turn immortalized in a concept, then, only then does drinking (and not the making of drinks) become an art. Making a drink is instead technique and obviously to express these concepts Donn implemented his technique, taking inspiration from Constante. A technique to emphasize the most hidden nature of the ingredients in the glass and, in particular, the evolution of aged rums.

The exotic cocktail was not born by chance but is the result of a technical elaboration without equal and of the study not only of mixing but of the entire social context that Donn, through the cocktail, has supported and with foresight has then directed towards the epochal change brought by the Tiki Era.

It is for this reason that Donn's cocktails have their own precise meaning and address in each of their peculiarities, from the name, to the type of balance, to the ingredients. Nothing, absolutely nothing, is left to chance.

The customer who drinks a Donn cocktail is first of all involved in a state of mind, he drinks to go along with it, to emphasize it or to immerse himself in it. The taste, the aroma of the drink is undoubtedly influenced by this mental state and vice versa. When the concept intrinsic to cocktails disappeared over the years, Tiki died, the value of the cocktail was exclusively related to its quality and a low quality, together with a non-existent content, made most of the cocktails of that time disappear.

On the contrary, the drinks which expressed this value in a stronger way have been immortalized in history independently from the quality and the change of social values. Such as the Zombie, the Mai Tai etc.

TIPS FOR TIKI COCKTAIL TWISTS

In conclusion, if today we still remember and drink many of these drinks, even without knowing they belong to the Tiki era, it is because they have been contextualized and the concept expressed has kept them alive even when the ingredients with which they were made have failed or have become poor. So my advice in making Tiki cocktail twists is to respect this concept both when we want to replicate a drink from the era and when we want to create a new drink.

That is, in making Tiki cocktail twists, in principle we can also change many of the ingredients to alter or add flavors, but it is important that the purpose and concept remain the same. The customer drinking a tiki must immerse themselves in a state of mind and that is not easy, but nothing that is noteworthy has ever been easy. Of course one can absolutely drink a drink just because it is good, but undoubtedly tastes and fashions are more fickle than the mind, than emotions.

If this were not the case we would all continue to drink crushed cuba, havana 7 and cola and the long island would be the ultimate drink and it is good when it tastes like peach tea. I don't think anyone has the ambition to change an entire society with a drink and maybe Donn didn't either, and he did. But it's undeniable that, in the smallness of one's own bar, indulging this conceptual peculiarity for one, two, ten, customers means somehow retaining them over time. Donn has "retained" entire generations.

During the courses I always give the example of the martini cocktail drinker both in terms of the concept and the taste of the drink. A martini cocktail is never drunk at random, it is not a spritz, the martini drinker knows what he drinks, knows how he wants it even without knowing what is in it or the techniques to make it, but knows how he feels and how he wants to feel in that moment in relation to his martini cocktail. And when he finds a bartender who satisfies this singular and subjective habit, he becomes a regular.

Here try replacing his martini cocktail with a twist, maybe one of those American apple martini type cocktails. I don't think you'll see that again at the bar.

So, if a customer asks for a '34 Zombie he expects a '34 Zombie, not a double, triple, quadruple drink in a 60cl cup. A tip for novices is that to make drinks, all drinks, you have to study, even more so to make twists or twists of tiki cocktails. Recipes are useful, but they are only the practical indication to put into practice what has been studied. And in fact they always need to be interpreted and it is done with knowledge.

In the next chapter I will talk about ingredients and techniques, about what I think is the correct way to reinterpret or create twists of tiki cocktails and maybe invent new ones.

TIKI COCKTAIL INGREDIENTS

Regardless of the ingredients of Tiki cocktails, as I mentioned in the previous chapter, many of these cocktails, thanks to their conceptual expression, especially those of Don the Beachcomber's mixing, have acquired a strong identity and have survived time, fashions and even the lack of the original ingredients. This value of the drink, embellished by the search for taste, meets people's feelings and is so important that it has been immediately replicated and imitated.

Despite the fact that Donn cared a great deal about the confidentiality of the ingredients of the Tiki cocktails in his recipes, after a very short time, dozens of his drinks, with names completely similar to the original ones were repurposed in the bars of Hollywood, where it all began, and then replicated all over the United States and the world. No one but Donn had any idea what was in a Missionary's Downfall, a Doctor Funk, Q.B. Cooler, a Pearl Diver, a Sumatra Kula, etc.

However with the exception of some drinks such as the Zombie, which immediately became a classic and everyone will always know by the name of Zombie, preparations with different cocktail ingredients but with names similar to the original ones such as Missionary's Doom, Doctor Chan, Dr. Fong, K.O. Cooler, Deep Sea Diver, Cuba Kula, etc. were born everywhere.

Any bartender could have invented cocktails with original names and ingredients in Tiki style, maybe even banal ones with passion fruit, pineapple and some random rum and in part, not knowing the original recipes, they did it but they hardly remained in the memory, because of the lack of a context. What is curious and makes us think about ingredients, is that necessarily all bartenders who approached this new trend had to make up for the lack of information and adapt themselves in mixing and balancing, but, as for the names and the service of these new creations or replicas, they all wanted to draw from the original idea of Donn's drinks.

This choice is obviously attributable to the need of recalling those sensations, those feelings, those desires that people needed, therefore the recall to the very sense of the drink that by now customers identified in Donn's exotic potions. Expressive sensations had already outclassed the research of taste in relation to the ingredients of Tiki cocktails and this immediately guaranteed the popularity of the cocktail itself. So all these new drinks with names recalling the originals were presented to the customer with the same serving glass used by Donn, the same color and precisely a name recalling the now popular starting drink.

Finally, with the exception of Donn's former employees, the Filipinos, who acquired technical knowledge and intuition about the ingredients of the Tiki recipes so they could also invent new cocktails and make twists of the original ones, most of the bartenders created many non-contextualized drinks and twists that today are no longer remembered.

The ingredients of Tiki cocktails.

Tiki mixing, as I have already said, is divided in various phases and, in relation to these, many tend to classify the ingredients of Tiki recipes by distinguishing them according to periods. From my point of view this can be correct only if we want to give it a purely historical and temporal meaning but absolutely useless in order to understand the balances of these blends, even in perspective of a twist or new cocktails.

What makes these cocktails identifiable is a precise style, technique and concept expressed which I have long talked about, no matter the origin of the ingredients of the tiki cocktail. Obviously Donn in 1930 created cocktails suited to the way of drinking but also of living of the society of that time, therefore static, powerful, complex and if we want meditative cocktails.

For this reason Donn never used fresh fruit but only processed fruit, certainly to ensure a longer shelf-life but most of all to obtain an aromatic concentration as high and optimized as possible in order to be explosive at every sip. Despite this prerogative, when some ingredients were missing, the only way to get them was to go and get them in person. When the sign "Gone to the Island" was posted on the door of Don the Beachcomber, it was a sign that Donn had closed the bar to go to Hawaii to retrieve the ingredients for the Tiki recipes.

The primary, indispensable and necessary ingredients for Donn's drinks are rums. The rest are "accessories", complementary, that is used to aromatize, balance and even just to harmonize colors. We can say that the ingredients of many of Donn's tiki cocktails, in relation to aromas, have practically the same function as bitters and sugar in the old fashioned. To enhance, balance, improve and bring in aromas, it is no coincidence that this style, this technique, has been so important to mixing since the beginning of cocktail history. *But are we sure that if Donn had tropical, oriental, European fruits etc. at his disposal, he would not have used them?*

I believe he would have, I'm convinced that if, as we do today, he regularly had available mango, peaches, pears, lychee, yuzu etc. from the Bengali's below he would have used any ingredient. That doesn't mean, however, that he would have created fruit cocktails. Surely, in the same way of passion fruit, which he regularly used, he would have processed these products in order to be able to guarantee the result I mentioned before, obviously always in relation to rum.

UNDERSTANDING TIKI COCKTAILS TO TWIST THEM

Every cocktail worth its salt has a reason that justifies its existence and its resistance to time, this reason is expressed through the technique and processing of the ingredients of tiki recipes. Understanding the meaning of the drink helps us to recreate a way of drinking, a style, and therefore to make twists. For this reason I believe there are no aromas that are good and aromas that are not good, all the possible ingredients of the cocktail must be processed in order to obtain the technical result adequate to the sense.

Not always but, especially in the most important Tiki mixes, with the possible exception of some sporadic cocktails which are known for their image and period, the identification of the drinks can be determined by a certain predominance of style dictated by the author. This reiterated style, "the bartender's pulse," often traces a new line of mixing or even initiates and identifies a historical period independent of the ingredients in Tiki recipes. In that case, this logic of style, the signature of the author then, is also present in each different category of the drink. As the Tiki culture has been so absorbing that it has become part of the habits of an entire society and in all its aspects, even the oldest mixes and categories of drinks, including the most classic and ancient ones, are adapted to Tiki but the best reinterpretations of them will always be referable to a precise style, often dictated by the founding fathers. Therefore there can be cocktails such as julep, sour, old fashioned, hot punch etc. contextualized in the Tiki period and characterized by a style determined by the author.

Hot punch, coffee grog, hot buttered or drinks served after a meal for example, are however part of these blends even though they are different categories and styles from the usual ones we are used to know today about Tiki. Therefore we can also find the same ingredients but processed with different techniques in order to express different results. In order to better explain this concept the only way is to give examples of ingredients of tiki cocktails.

SAMPLE PROCESSING OF TIKI COCKTAIL INGREDIENTS

Let's start with the most talked about, coconut in Tiki mixing. Donn never uses coconut in his drinks, except for a home made coconut cream, since the first industrial coconut cream, Coco Lopez, did not exist yet. But it is important to notice that its use is exclusively relegated to hot punches, such as Tiger's Milk.

The spreading and popularity of Pina Colada at the end of the 50's, in the middle of the Tiki era, contributed to confuse different styles. Even today it is erroneously spread the belief that Pina Colada is a Tiki cocktail and so is the ingredient coconut in Tiki recipes. The reason why it is never used is simple, coconut cream is oily and sweet and moreover in modest quantities it does not have particularly strong aromas which cannot be overpowered by sweetness. As opposed to the recurring almond for horchata, in particular bitter almond, processed coconut does not have the same pungency and aromatic capacity in proportion to sweetness and quantities used. Not surprisingly, what made Pina Colada an obsolete drink was the difficulty in balancing it which erroneously led to the belief that it was a sweet drink, therefore not suitable for all palates.

Coconut water (fresh) instead, however not easily available, would be too little intense and would dilute Donn's drink too much and would irremediably destructure it in regard to its purpose. In Donn's use, instead, coconut cream is perfect to be substituted or to be added in good quantity to butter in a hot buttered drink, giving aroma, exalted by the heat of the cocktail, sweetness and texture. Even Trader Vic does not use coconut cream in his cocktails, as it is not particularly suited for his very fresh and acid drinks.

In any case, according to my way of interpreting Tiki mixing, in this particular example with reference to Donn, I do not feel to exclude a priori the ingredient "coconut" just because Donn did not use it. Granted that to my personal taste it is not an aroma that I like very much, today however there are many other innovative techniques to extract the aromas and process them to adapt the ingredients of the recipes.

Therefore if we have the rotating space sonicator or the evaporating halberd with proton rays used by Daitarn III, Jeeg Robot, and Cern in Geneva, we can find a way to enhance an aroma by excluding the other characteristics which would be detrimental to the drink. In the case of coconut, obviously the fat part.

In this sense we can use countless aromas and therefore make many twists by selecting new products and therefore different from the ingredients of the original tiki cocktails, while maintaining the sense of the cocktail and perhaps the style of the author we want to replicate. Already at that time Donn himself understood the meaning of processing his ingredients in tiki recipes in relation to aromas. There are fatty preparations with blends of aromas which are exceptional, just think about the simple Coola Culla Mix or the legendary Gardenia Mix.

But as I said before their use in these blends, because of the excessive fatty part, would negatively influence the cocktail. When Donn decides to use the flavors of the exceptional Gardenia Mix (a buttery preparation designed for hot buttered) in a cold drink such as the Pearl Diver he works it in a different way. From these heavy ingredients of Tiki cocktails the fat part is excluded keeping instead the aromas in the cocktail. By dosing the ice in a different way and by filtering it, it degreases the whole drink after having chilled it, practically with a simple technique which is frequently used today and known as fat wash. Ingenious technique if we think he applied an instant fat wash on the drink in the 30's.

In the next chapter I will talk more about twists by making examples with ingredients and cocktails in order to try to understand the meaning of drinks and to be able to adapt the ingredients of tiki cocktails.

TIKI COCKTAIL TWISTS EXAMPLES

In this chapter I will give examples of Tiki cocktail twists as the last part inherent to the theme of twists. In particular in this chapter I will talk about practical examples by analyzing three very different drinks but among the most known and famous ones from Donn Beach. The Don's Special Daiquiri, the Missionary's Downfall and the Zombie.

FIRST EXAMPLE: DON'S SPECIAL DAIQUIRI

Drink by now very famous, one of the first Tiki drinks to be nowadays reproduced in bars by those who approach this mixing. The reason is not so much to be found in its ease of reproduction as in the composition of its aromas that can satisfy most palates. Let's say the truth, with honey and passion fruit it is never wrong, but be careful! If not correctly balanced it could end up like those cocktails with pineapple all the same which at the end of the 60's decreed the end of Tiki mixing.

I chose this as one of the examples of Tiki cocktail twists because Don's Special Daiquiri is not a honey and passion fruit drink but it is always a rum drink enriched by aromas such as honey and passion fruit. In order to understand the balance, as I widely expressed in the previous articles, it is necessary to study the cocktail in its essence.

Don's Special was born with the name of Mona Daiquiri. That is a Daiquiri style drink, created with a now legendary rum such as Myers's Mona.

Mona was Jamaican rum over 20 years old that made this drink "special", the absolute protagonist. As it often happened in that period not always the production of rum could be constant, indeed some times as in this case, or in the case of the legendary Wray & Nephew 17 years of Mai Tai or the Dagger themselves, some products ceased to exist or even changed significantly to according to the market of the country where it was exported.

Once Mona 20 years old rum was no longer available, Donn had to use other rums finding a solution in order not to lose the sense of the cocktail and therefore necessarily had to change its name. As Donn did, only by replacing the Myers's Mona with another rum as special and caretterizzante we can create a twist of the original drink, with a rum that can emerge and enhance together with the aromas of honey and passion fruit.

The sense of this Special Daiquiri is still witnessed by Mariano Licudine's version of the drink. Licudine bases his mixing just on the replication of Donn's drinks and gives us many examples of twist of Tiki cocktails. The Filipino disciple of Donn, proposes to Mai Kai a version of his own but, not being able to call it with the name of Donn, let alone with that of Mona rum, he simply calls it Special Daiquiri. To support this thesis there are evidences that indicate Special Daiquiri and Don's Special Daiquiri were also called respectively Special Reserve Daiquiri and Don's Special Reserve Daiquiri. Obviously the word Reserve is used to indicate the particularity of the rum used.

So if we were to use, as it often happens today, rums with little character, such as light white rums or soft and sweet amber rums, we would easily lose the distillate by creating a honey and passion fruit drink instead of rum. My advice, if you want to use honey and passion fruit as in the original recipe, is to use a rather dry rum, aged, with a high alcohol content. The soft texture of honey would dampen the tannic part of a rum that could be too intrusive but at the same time widen the aromatic palette. Passion syrup as well as giving smoothness and sweetness would, with further acidity added to lime, exalt the most subdued notes of rum such as the ones given by wood or even the wood itself maybe of a particular cask or a particularly toasted cask.

The alcohol by volume would also support the most volatile and fresh notes that in a context of such imported aromas could be easily lost. Not always only one rum can, in blending, support and stand for all this, it is not impossible but in lack of such a "special" rum, for this reason, Donn invented the exotic blending with more rums together balanced ad hoc for every drink. So starting with a rum that will make our Daiquiri a Daiquiri Special, we can also build our own twist by substituting complementary cocktail ingredients.

Can we replace the passion fruit with another syrup? Sure.

If through another flavor, perhaps one of our home made, we can balance sweetness and acidity in relation to the rum or blend of rums that we want to enhance, we can do so. I still remember that the drink was called Mona Daiquiri, then Don's Special Reserve Daiquiri and never called Don's Honey Daquiri or Don's Special Passion Daiquiri, the protagonist is the rum, what must be special is always and only the rum! In respect of what has been said therefore a twist will no longer be Don's Special Daiquiri never Our Special Daiquiri. In case of reproduction of the original Don's Special we will use honey and passion fruit but with a rum or a blend suitable to be the protagonist as explained before.

SECOND EXAMPLE: MISSIONARY'S DOWNFALL

Donn rarely made cocktails with pineapple, even though in some books you have read about tropical pineapple being shipped to California, true, but Donn used pineapple juice more frequently only starting from the 50's, when he changed his mixing style adapting to the times. Pineapple was the easiest tropical fruit to find, process and in time industrially packaged in juices or concentrates, this explains its wide diffusion especially in concomitance with the birth of tourism in the mid 50's. It was the undisputed protagonist with industrial preparations even in the period of decadence of Tiki mixing after the 60's. There are dozens of examples of twists of tiki cocktails with pineapple completely unbalanced that followed the fashion without any sense of mixing. But going back to the 30'/40's, to Donn's first mixing, we can understand that he did not frequently use fresh juice to create long drinks with pineapple, not only from the recipes themselves, but by analyzing the balance of them in relation to the size of the drinks made.

Therefore it is not enough to know that Donn used pineapple to use pineapple juice indiscriminately in every drink or twist referring to Donn, in fact most of the old Donn drinks with few cl of pineapple juice would lose their structure. This does not mean that with a proper processing of the raw material, in order to extract the aroma while maintaining the structure of the cocktail, we cannot use pineapple and twist even old drinks. Like passion fruit in Don's Special in order to create a cocktail with pineapple we must use it and process it in the correct way. As an example, intensifying the juice or a syrup and why not acidifying it slightly, couldn't we substitute it for the passion fruit syrup that maybe we use to make a Don's Special that I mentioned before? I would say yes if we respect the balance and the sense of which I spoke before.

We can say that today's version of the original cocktail is indeed one of the examples of Tiki cocktail twists, maybe not properly wanted but due to needs. Few people know that the ingredients of the Missionary's Downfall cocktail are from the very beginning intentionally skewed towards sweet. It took me years to understand why this drink was so different from all the others prepared by Donn. Different in technique, in balance, in aromas, so much so as to make it unique and make it seem like a drink not his own.

I was able to understand the meaning of this preparation only by studying all the old menus of that time, both the originals of Don the Beachcomber and all the ones that reproposed the twist of this drink trying to copy or to draw from Donn's work. I understood its essence and its evolution only when I realized that in the old menus it was not positioned next to the sections of the various Zombies, Navy Grog, Beachcomber Gold, Test Pilot etc. but it was inserted together with the hot buttered, coffee grog, hot punch and other invigorating drinks which were served after a meal. Missionary's Downfall was indeed, one of the few cocktails with pineapple, a drink which tended to be sweeter but above all very smooth and velvety, evidently proposed as an after meal or maybe just as a replacement for a dessert, its texture reminds and must remind more a Rum Cow rather than a classic drink. Today I have never seen anyone serving the drink in this way, modern mixing and our culture far from the ordinary consumption of toddy has made Missionary's Downfall to be consequently rebalanced with an acid tone and therefore more suitable to our times, although keeping the same texture, the same smoothness that pineapple naturally guarantees.

As a matter of fact, even with regard to the technique used today to make Missionary's Downfall, I have reason to believe it is not the same used to make the drink but the one through which it physiologically evolved.

I am convinced that Donn's first Missionary's Downfall was made with the Milkshake Mixer. From the testimonies it seems that the drink is one of the first cocktails invented by Donn, born in the 30' 40' era in which Donn had already widely implemented his mixing technique with the milkshake mixer. A basic tool, fundamental and indispensable for all his mixing and that Donn will never replace with the new miracle mixer Waring Blendor. Waring Blendor, a tool I remember patented not as a mixer but as a disintegrator and that was its function. Even the pictures of the original menus, which faithfully reproduce the cocktails served at Don the Beachcomber, show the Missionary's Downfall served in a classic cocktail glass

This serving in a cup, as we know, would be impossible with the modern production of the drink, in fact just the solid parts whipped and then the excessive foam need a glass larger than the double cup.

On the other hand, I am of the opinion that proposing a Missionary's Downfall with the original technique and in a cup, even rebalanced on acidity, could open the drink to new aromatic nuances and at the same time give it the extreme elegance of a drink in a cup as well as the spectacularity of one of those drinks with "artistic personalization" in a cup with velvet that we are used to see today and that are very fashionable.   In my opinion it could be a good solution as an example of the twist of Tiki cocktails strictly anchored to history as well.

Instead of pineapple we could easily use other fruits and instead of mint other fresh aromatic herbs. But as it generates much less foam than the one pineapple naturally creates in the process, we could use more "mellow" and sweet fruit such as a peach or mango puree and add an aromatic velvet. For example a fresh and aromatic Mediterranean herb that I really like is nepitella that we could substitute for mint or even create a velvet.

THIRD EXAMPLE: THE ZOMBIE

The 1934 Zombie is one of Donn's most complex drinks but again we need to understand the concept within the drink. The one and only reason why the Zombie is one of the most famous drinks in mixing history is because of its extreme balance. Balance with which Donn was able to mask the great alcoholic power that, at the expense of perception, is able to surprise the customer in its effects and in the concentration of aromas.

Obviously, some marketing ideas, the replicas of other clubs, and the stories related to the mythical drink contributed to its popularity but at the base there is an impressive study in order to guarantee a quality product. The Zombie has the power of 5 modern cocktails (considering 4.5 cl. of distillate per drink) a power that however is hidden in a single glass and not a big glass but a tube tumbler, the classic Collins, of only about 33cl.

The Zombie of 1934 cannot and should not be served in a Tiki mug. Only after the 50's the glasses will be bigger because the new Zombie will change both in technique and in recipe, as I said before there will be many Zombies that will be cocktails with pineapple. What I always say in my courses is that the Zombie is not a double, triple, quadruple drink in a half-liter cup but a normal drink in a standard glass.

Now try to drink a normal gin and tonic with more than 2 oz of gin, a cuba libre with 2, 3 oz of rum, they become undrinkable because they are unbalanced, too strong despite the large amount of non-alcoholic soda in the drink. Zombie contains 5 oz of rum or better 3oz plus 1 oz of overproof 75° which would be equivalent to 2 oz of a normal line rum at 37,5° plus falernum, pernod and angostura (click here for the recipe).

The non-alcoholic parts are almost irrelevant if we take out just a few ml of grapefruit juice from the Don's Mix and some lime. The Zombie is a pure concentrate of rum which must be able to surprise the customer first of all at an aromatic level, a drink studied and perfected for a long time by Donn through the technique of Constantino Ribalaigua, thanks to which it is able to mask the power of alcohol as well.

Unfortunately because of the difficult balance and the scarce technical knowledge, Zombie of 1934 is one of the most mistaken examples of Tiki cocktail twists. Let's be clear "Zombie is not lemonade" is however a strong drink, it is not that by making it properly it magically becomes a non-alcoholic drink but it is drinkable as opposed to the unbalanced gin and tonics I mentioned before and most of all it is good! The ingredients of Zombie cocktails are mainly alcoholic, of course, but we can choose our blend of rums as we like in order to get the aromatic composition we want to express, according to the power of the drink and the non alcoholic flavors we want to use to accompany it. The extreme balance of Zombie is visible to the naked eye, a static drink, perfectly uniform even in the fullness of its color. This, in the original recipe is the role of one of the ingredients such as grenadine.

It is unthinkable to think that 2 barspoons of grenadine in all that aromatic explosion could influence in a decisive way the taste of the drink. In this case grenadine, besides giving texture and a slight sweetness, has more the function of harmonizing and filling the color. In some drinks this function was even primary, very characteristic, such as in Doctor Funk. In the Zombie described before, matcha tea syrup had this function as well, even though it was more aromatic than grenadine.

With these simple examples of Tiki cocktail twists I wanted to give tangible proof that even though Tiki drinks, in particular Donn's, are no longer replicable in the absence of the exact same ingredients they can still be reproduced and even twisted. But it is necessary to pay attention to the processing of ingredients, we have seen that even to make a cocktail with pineapple there can be countless processing with opposite results. The reproduction and the twist is possible because the value of these drinks, as I have always said, goes beyond the search for taste but it is very conceptual. Concepts in my opinion extremely current or adaptable to today's world expressed by particular techniques that make Donn one of the few innovative bartenders of this work.

The quantity of products on the market today, from fruit to rums, is in my opinion remarkable and higher than at that time, even qualitatively higher, as well as the processing techniques of the same have improved. This is the reason why if you respect traditions and concepts, which are then the sense of the drink itself, there are no limits in the reproduction of drinks of that time as well as in the creation of new ones.

BOOK 5
COCKTAIL RECIPES

CLASSIC RECIPES

Welcome to the world of classic cocktails, where the art of mixology is celebrated and cherished. This cookbook is a guide to some of the most iconic cocktails in history, from the Maple Old Fashioned to the Honey Sage Margarita, and everything in between.

This cookbook is more than just a collection of recipes. It's a journey through the history of cocktails, exploring the stories and traditions that have made these drinks so beloved. It's a journey through the evolution of mixology, from the speakeasies of the Prohibition era to the modern craft cocktail movement. And it's a journey through the creativity and innovation of bartenders and mixologists around the world, who continue to push the boundaries of what is possible with cocktails. Whether you're a seasoned mixologist or a cocktail enthusiast just starting out, this cookbook is a celebration of the art and craft of cocktail-making.

BLACKBERRY MINT JULEP

The Blackberry Mint Julep is a refreshing twist on the classic cocktail. The addition of blackberries and mint gives it a fruity and herbaceous flavor that's perfect for sipping on a warm summer day.

INGREDIENTS:

- 2 oz. bourbon
- 1 oz. blackberry syrup
- 3-4 fresh mint leaves
- Crushed ice
- Mint sprig and blackberries, for garnish

INSTRUCTIONS:

1. In a mixing glass, muddle the mint leaves and blackberry syrup.
2. Add the bourbon and stir until well combined.
3. Fill a glass with crushed ice.
4. Strain the mixture over the ice.
5. Garnish with a mint sprig and fresh blackberries.

MAPLE OLD FASHIONED

The Maple Old Fashioned is a cozy and comforting twist on the classic cocktail. The addition of maple syrup gives it a warm sweetness that's perfect for sipping on a cool evening.

INGREDIENTS:

- 2 oz. bourbon
- 1/2 oz. maple syrup
- 2 dashes Angostura bitters
- Orange peel, for garnish

INSTRUCTIONS:

1. In a mixing glass, stir together the bourbon, maple syrup, and bitters.
2. Fill a glass with ice.
3. Strain the mixture over the ice.
4. Garnish with a twist of orange peel.

GRAPEFRUIT NEGRONI

The Grapefruit Negroni is a bright and citrusy twist on the classic cocktail. The addition of grapefruit juice gives it a tart and refreshing flavor that's perfect for sipping on a warm evening.

INGREDIENTS:

- 1 oz. gin
- 1 oz. Campari
- 1 oz. sweet vermouth
- 1 oz. fresh grapefruit juice
- Grapefruit twist, for garnish

INSTRUCTIONS:

1. In a mixing glass, stir together the gin, Campari, sweet vermouth, and grapefruit juice.
2. Fill a glass with ice.
3. Strain the mixture over the ice.
4. Garnish with a twist of grapefruit peel.

LAVENDER LEMON DROP

The Lavender Lemon Drop is a sophisticated twist on the classic cocktail that's perfect for sipping at a garden party. The addition of lavender simple syrup gives it a floral and delicate flavor.

INGREDIENTS:

- 2 oz. vodka
- 1 oz. fresh lemon juice

- 1/2 oz. lavender simple syrup
- Lemon twist, for garnish

INSTRUCTIONS:

1. In a shaker, combine the vodka, fresh lemon juice, and lavender simple syrup.
2. Shake vigorously for about 15 seconds.
3. Strain the mixture into a chilled glass.
4. Garnish with a lemon twist.

SPICED MANHATTAN

The Spiced Manhattan is a cozy and warming twist on the classic cocktail that's perfect for sipping on a cool evening. The addition of spiced simple syrup gives it a warm and spicy flavor.

INGREDIENTS:

- 2 oz. rye whiskey
- 1 oz. sweet vermouth
- 1/2 oz. spiced simple syrup
- Orange twist, for garnish

INSTRUCTIONS:

1. In a mixing glass, stir together the rye whiskey, sweet vermouth, and spiced simple syrup.
2. Fill a glass with ice.
3. Strain the mixture over the ice.
4. Garnish with a twist of orange peel.

GINGERBREAD OLD FASHIONED

The Gingerbread Old Fashioned is a festive twist on the classic cocktail that's perfect for the holiday season. The addition of gingerbread syrup gives it a warm and spicy flavor.

INGREDIENTS:

- 2 oz. bourbon
- 1/2 oz. gingerbread syrup
- 2 dashes Angostura bitters
- Orange peel and cinnamon stick, for garnish

INSTRUCTIONS:

1. In a mixing glass, stir together the bourbon, gingerbread syrup, and bitters.
2. Fill a glass with ice.
3. Strain the mixture over the ice.
4. Garnish with a twist of orange peel and a cinnamon stick.

ESPRESSO MARTINI

The Espresso Martini is a sophisticated twist on the classic cocktail that's perfect for coffee lovers. The addition of espresso gives it a rich and bold flavor.

INGREDIENTS:

- 2 oz. vodka
- 1 oz. freshly brewed espresso
- 1/2 oz. coffee liqueur
- 3 coffee beans, for garnish

INSTRUCTIONS:

1. Fill a shaker with ice.
2. Add the vodka, freshly brewed espresso, and coffee liqueur to the shaker.
3. Shake vigorously for about 15 seconds.
4. Strain the mixture into a chilled glass.
5. Garnish with three coffee beans.

ROSEMARY GIN FIZZ

The Rosemary Gin Fizz is a refreshing twist on the classic cocktail that's perfect for sipping on a warm day. The addition of rosemary gives it an herbaceous and refreshing flavor.

INGREDIENTS:

- 2 oz. gin
- 1 oz. fresh lemon juice
- 1/2 oz. rosemary simple syrup
- Club soda
- Rosemary sprig and lemon slice, for garnish

INSTRUCTIONS:

1. Fill a shaker with ice.
2. Add the gin, fresh lemon juice, and rosemary simple syrup to the shaker.
3. Shake vigorously for about 15 seconds.
4. Strain the mixture into a glass filled with ice.
5. Top with club soda.
6. Garnish with a sprig of rosemary and a slice of lemon.

HONEY SAGE MARGARITA

The Honey Sage Margarita is a sweet and savory twist on the classic cocktail. The addition of honey and sage gives it a complex and sophisticated flavor.

INGREDIENTS:

- 2 oz. tequila
- 1 oz. fresh lime juice
- 1/2 oz. honey syrup
- 2 sage leaves
- Salt and lime wedge, for garnish

INSTRUCTIONS:

1. In a shaker, muddle the sage leaves with the honey syrup.
2. Add the tequila and fresh lime juice to the shaker.
3. Fill the shaker with ice and shake vigorously for about 15 seconds.
4. Rim a glass with salt and fill with ice.
5. Strain the mixture over the ice in the glass.
6. Garnish with a lime wedge.

CINNAMON HOT TODDY

The Cinnamon Hot Toddy is a cozy and warming twist on the classic cocktail. The addition of cinnamon gives it a warm and spicy flavor that's perfect for sipping on a cold evening.

INGREDIENTS:

- 2 oz. bourbon

- 1/2 oz. honey
- 1 cinnamon stick
- Hot water
- Lemon twist, for garnish

INSTRUCTIONS:

1. In a mug, combine the bourbon, honey, and cinnamon stick.
2. Fill the mug with hot water and stir until the honey is dissolved.
3. Garnish with a lemon twist.

CHERRY AMARETTO SOUR

The Cherry Amaretto Sour is a fruity twist on the classic cocktail. The addition of cherry and amaretto gives it a sweet and nutty flavor that's perfect for sipping on a warm day.

INGREDIENTS:

- 2 oz. bourbon
- 1 oz. fresh lemon juice
- 1/2 oz. amaretto
- 1/2 oz. cherry syrup
- Maraschino cherry and lemon slice, for garnish

INSTRUCTIONS:

1. In a shaker, combine the bourbon, fresh lemon juice, amaretto, and cherry syrup.
2. Fill the shaker with ice and shake vigorously for about 15 seconds.
3. Fill a glass with ice.

4. Strain the mixture over the ice in the glass.

5. Garnish with a maraschino cherry and a slice of lemon.

SMOKED RECIPES

Welcome to the world of smoked cocktails, where the traditional art of mixology is infused with the bold and complex flavors of smoke. This cookbook is a guide to some of the most delicious and innovative smoked cocktails out there. From the classic Smoky Margarita to the more modern Smoke & Mirrors, you'll learn how to create these amazing cocktails in the comfort of your own home. Whether you're an experienced mixologist or just starting out, this cookbook is your passport to the smoky and delicious world of cocktail-making. So grab your shaker, your favorite spirits, and let's get smoking!

SMOKED WHISKEY SOUR

The Smoked Whiskey Sour is a classic cocktail with a smoky twist. The addition of smoke gives it a bold and complex flavor that's perfect for sipping on a cool evening.

INGREDIENTS:

- 2 oz. bourbon
- 1 oz. fresh lemon juice
- 1/2 oz. simple syrup
- Egg white
- Cedar wood chips

INSTRUCTIONS:

1. In a shaker, combine the bourbon, fresh lemon juice, simple syrup, and egg white.
2. Add a handful of cedar wood chips to a smoking gun and light them on fire.
3. Once the chips are smoking, place the hose of the smoking gun into the shaker and let the smoke fill the shaker for a few seconds.
4. Remove the hose from the shaker and add ice.
5. Shake vigorously for about 15 seconds.
6. Strain the mixture into a glass filled with ice.

SMOKY MARGARITA

The Smoky Margarita is a classic cocktail with a smoky twist. The addition of smoke and chili salt gives it a bold and complex flavor that's perfect for sipping on a warm day.

INGREDIENTS:

- 2 oz. tequila
- 1 oz. fresh lime juice
- 1/2 oz. agave nectar
- Cedar wood chips
- Chili salt

INSTRUCTIONS:

1. Rim a glass with chili salt.
2. Fill a shaker with ice and add the tequila, fresh lime juice, and agave nectar.
3. Add a handful of cedar wood chips to a smoking gun and light them on fire.

4. Once the chips are smoking, place the hose of the smoking gun into the shaker and let the smoke fill the shaker for a few seconds.

5. Remove the hose from the shaker and shake vigorously for about 15 seconds.

6. Strain the mixture into the rimmed glass filled with ice.

SMOKE & MIRRORS

The Smoke & Mirrors cocktail is a sophisticated twist on the classic cocktail. The addition of smoke and rosemary gives it a warm and herbaceous flavor that's perfect for sipping on a cool evening.

INGREDIENTS:

- 2 oz. gin
- 1 oz. fresh lemon juice
- 1/2 oz. honey syrup
- Egg white
- Rosemary sprig
- Cedar wood chips

INSTRUCTIONS:

1. In a shaker, combine the gin, fresh lemon juice, honey syrup, and egg white.

2. Add a handful of cedar wood chips to a smoking gun and light them on fire.

3. Once the chips are smoking, place the rosemary sprig in the shaker and the hose of the smoking gun into the shaker and let the smoke fill the shaker for a few seconds.

4. Remove the hose from the shaker and add ice.

5. Shake vigorously for about 15 seconds.

6. Strain the mixture into a glass filled with ice. Garnish with a rosemary sprig.

SMOKED MAPLE OLD FASHIONED

The Smoked Maple Old Fashioned is a smoky twist on the classic cocktail that's perfect for sipping on a cool evening. The addition of maple syrup gives it a warm and sweet flavor.

INGREDIENTS:

- 2 oz. bourbon
- 1/2 oz. maple syrup
- 2 dashes Angostura bitters
- Orange peel
- Applewood wood chips

INSTRUCTIONS:

1. In a mixing glass, stir together the bourbon, maple syrup, and bitters.
2. Add a handful of applewood wood chips to a smoking gun and light them on fire.
3. Once the chips are smoking, place the hose of the smoking gun into the mixing glass and let the smoke fill the glass for a few seconds.
4. Remove the hose from the mixing glass and add ice.
5. Stir for about 15 seconds.
6. Strain the mixture into a glass filled with ice.
7. Garnish with an orange peel.

SMOKED CHOCOLATE MARTINI

The Smoked Chocolate Martini is a decadent twist on the classic cocktail that's perfect for dessert. The addition of chocolate bitters and smoke gives it a rich and complex flavor.

INGREDIENTS:

- 2 oz. vodka
- 1 oz. Godiva chocolate liqueur
- 2 dashes chocolate bitters
- Cedar wood chips

INSTRUCTIONS:

1. Fill a shaker with ice and add the vodka, Godiva chocolate liqueur, and chocolate bitters.
2. Add a handful of cedar wood chips to a smoking gun and light them on fire.
3. Once the chips are smoking, place the hose of the smoking gun into the shaker and let the smoke fill the shaker for a few seconds.
4. Remove the hose from the shaker and shake vigorously for about 15 seconds.
5. Strain the mixture into a chilled martini glass.

SMOKED GRAPEFRUIT MARGARITA

The Smoked Grapefruit Margarita is a refreshing twist on the classic cocktail that's perfect for sipping on a warm day. The addition of grapefruit and smoke gives it a bright and complex flavor.

INGREDIENTS:

- 2 oz. tequila
- 1 oz. fresh grapefruit juice
- 1/2 oz. fresh lime juice
- 1/2 oz. agave nectar
- Grapefruit slice
- Mesquite wood chips

INSTRUCTIONS:

1. Rim a glass with salt.
2. Fill a shaker with ice and add the tequila, fresh grapefruit juice, fresh lime juice, and agave nectar.
3. Add a handful of mesquite wood chips to a smoking gun and light them on fire.
4. Once the chips are smoking, place the grapefruit slice in the shaker and the hose of the smoking gun into the shaker and let the smoke fill the shaker for a few seconds.
5. Remove the hose from the shaker and shake vigorously for about 15 seconds.
6. Strain the mixture into the rimmed glass filled with ice.

SMOKED PINEAPPLE MARGARITA

The Smoked Pineapple Margarita is a tropical twist on the classic cocktail that's perfect for sipping on a warm day. The addition of smoked pineapple gives it a sweet and tangy flavor.

INGREDIENTS:

- 2 oz. tequila
- 1 oz. fresh pineapple juice
- 1/2 oz. fresh lime juice
- 1/2 oz. agave nectar
- Pineapple slice
- Cherry wood chips

INSTRUCTIONS:

1. Rim a glass with salt.
2. Fill a shaker with ice and add the tequila, fresh pineapple juice, fresh lime juice, and agave nectar.
3. Add a handful of cherry wood chips to a smoking gun and light them on fire.
4. Once the chips are smoking, place the pineapple slice in the shaker and the hose of the smoking gun into the shaker and let the smoke fill the shaker for a few seconds.
5. Remove the hose from the shaker and shake vigorously for about 15 seconds.
6. Strain the mixture into the rimmed glass filled with ice.

SMOKY MANHATTAN

The Smoky Manhattan is a sophisticated twist on the classic cocktail that's perfect for sipping on a cool evening. The addition of smoke and black walnut bitters gives it a rich and complex flavor.

INGREDIENTS:

- 2 oz. rye whiskey
- 1 oz. sweet vermouth

- 2 dashes black walnut bitters
- Orange peel
- Oak wood chips

INSTRUCTIONS:

1. Fill a mixing glass with ice and add the rye whiskey, sweet vermouth, and black walnut bitters.
2. Add a handful of oak wood chips to a smoking gun and light them on fire.
3. Once the chips are smoking, place the hose of the smoking gun into the mixing glass and let the smoke fill the glass for a few seconds.
4. Remove the hose from the mixing glass and stir for about 15 seconds.
5. Strain the mixture into a glass filled with ice.
6. Garnish with an orange peel.

SMOKED BLOODY MARY

The Smoked Bloody Mary is a smoky twist on the classic cocktail that's perfect for brunch. The addition of smoke and spicy pickled vegetables gives it a bold and complex flavor.

INGREDIENTS:

- 2 oz. vodka
- 4 oz. tomato juice
- 1/2 oz. fresh lemon juice
- 1 tsp. Worcestershire sauce
- Hot sauce, to taste
- Spicy pickled vegetables (e.g. pickled green beans, okra, etc.)

- Alder wood chips

INSTRUCTIONS:

1. Fill a shaker with ice and add the vodka, tomato juice, fresh lemon juice, Worcestershire sauce, and hot sauce.

2. Add a handful of alder wood chips to a smoking gun and light them on fire.

3. Once the chips are smoking, place the hose of the smoking gun into the shaker and let the smoke fill the shaker for a few seconds.

4. Remove the hose from the shaker and shake vigorously for about 15 seconds.

5. Strain the mixture into a glass filled with ice.

6. Garnish with spicy pickled vegetables.

SMOKY ESPRESSO MARTINI

The Smoky Espresso Martini is a rich and complex twist on the classic cocktail that's perfect for after dinner. The addition of smoke and espresso gives it a bold and delicious flavor.

INGREDIENTS:

- 2 oz. vodka
- 1 oz. freshly brewed espresso
- 1/2 oz. Kahlua
- 1/2 oz. simple syrup
- Coffee beans
- Hickory wood chips

INSTRUCTIONS:

1. Fill a shaker with ice and add the vodka, freshly brewed espresso, Kahlua, and simple syrup.
2. Add a handful of hickory wood chips to a smoking gun and light them on fire.
3. Once the chips are smoking, place the hose of the smoking gun into the shaker and let the smoke fill the shaker for a few seconds.
4. Remove the hose from the shaker and shake vigorously for about 15 seconds.
5. Strain the mixture into a chilled martini glass.
6. Garnish with coffee beans.

SMOKED CHERRY MANHATTAN

The Smoked Cherry Manhattan is a delicious twist on the classic cocktail that's perfect for sipping on a cool evening. The addition of smoke and cherry bitters gives it a rich and complex flavor.

INGREDIENTS:

- 2 oz. bourbon
- 1 oz. sweet vermouth
- 2 dashes cherry bitters
- Maraschino cherry
- Pecan wood chips

INSTRUCTIONS:

1. Fill a mixing glass with ice and add the bourbon, sweet vermouth, and cherry bitters.
2. Add a handful of pecan wood chips to a smoking gun and light them on fire.
3. Once the chips are smoking, place the hose of the smoking gun into the mixing glass and let the smoke fill the glass for a few seconds.

4. Remove the hose from the mixing glass and stir for about 15 seconds.
5. Strain the mixture into a glass filled with ice.
6. Garnish with a maraschino cherry.

SMOKED GRAPEFRUIT PALOMA

The Smoked Grapefruit Paloma is a refreshing twist on the classic cocktail that's perfect for sipping on a warm day. The addition of smoked grapefruit gives it a sweet and tangy flavor.

INGREDIENTS:

- 2 oz. tequila
- 1 oz. fresh grapefruit juice
- 1/2 oz. fresh lime juice
- 1/2 oz. agave nectar
- Grapefruit wedge
- Mesquite wood chips

INSTRUCTIONS:

1. Rim a glass with salt.
2. Fill a shaker with ice and add the tequila, fresh grapefruit juice, fresh lime juice, and agave nectar.
3. Add a handful of mesquite wood chips to a smoking gun and light them on fire.
4. Once the chips are smoking, place the grapefruit wedge in the shaker and the hose of the smoking gun into the shaker and let the smoke fill the shaker for a few seconds.
5. Remove the hose from the shaker and shake vigorously for about 15 seconds.
6. Strain the mixture into the rimmed glass filled with ice.

TIKI RECIPES

When talking about tiki cocktails or tiki drinks, the very popular mugs depicting different tiki idols inspired by Polynesian deities cannot fail to come to mind. Exotic scents, colors and flavors are mixed in tiki cocktails with a precise technique that finds its roots in the equally well-known daiquiri. Born in America in the 1930's, tiki drinks are cocktails made with an almost maniacal precision as their balance must be perfect in order to exalt distillates with spices and fresh fruits. Tiki mixing is a historical mixing but always evolving. Cocktails therefore can vary from the classics of the cocktail list of tiki bars of Don The Beachcomber to those of Trader Vic. But at the same time in addition to the two best known styles you can find recipes of other bartenders among the most influential and most popular tiki bars of the Tiki era. Also will be included some recipes of what is called the Modern Tiki. That is today's drinks of bartenders and fans of tiki mixing who experiment and work with this style but not necessarily have a completely tiki cocktail list.

MISSIONARY'S DOWNFALL

INGREDIENTS

- 1/2 oz Lime Juice
- 1 oz Honey Mix
- 1/2 oz Peach Brandy
- 1 oz Light Traditional Rum, smooth
- 3 or 4 whole pineapple chunks
- about ten mint leaves

The original recipe for Missionary's Downfall calls for the use of Peach Brandy, a product that as we know has been out of business for years. Conventionally Peach Brandy has been substituted with peach liqueur, which is obviously not the same thing.

Technique

Blended. Place all ingredients in the blender bell and blend, including mint! Yes...it is very strange but with proper balancing the result is very pleasing.

Service

Large cup. (like the classic brandy one). Serving the original Missionary's Downfall recipe with the first technique adopted requires a classic cocktail glass.

Secrets of proper making

The trick to making a good Missionary's Downfall with this recipe is to properly dose the ice.

I prefer to use crushed ice in the amount of less than half a bar scoop, so about 4 oz of crushed ice. With this Missionary's Downfall recipe the result should be like a smoothie so very smooth and it is necessary that the ice is completely disintegrated and dissolved. For this reason a classic blender is used.

Otherwise a layer of ice water would form and in time it would melt and get between the cocktail and the foam. This is the point where the solid blended parts will easily float. In any case, with time the drink, produced with this technique, will inevitably separate but with a correct technique we will slow down this time considerably.

We will realize a good realization when the drink will be soft and compact without any solid part in evidence and it will be positioned in the glass in two layers, the drink and its foam. If after a while another layer will form between the foam and the cocktail, it means the ice was too much and therefore not completely dissolved.

EASTERN SOUR COCKTAIL

INGREDIENTS

- 3/4 oz Lemon Juice (fresh)
- 2 1/2 oz Orange Juice (fresh)

- 1/4 oz Barley
- 1/4 oz Liquid Sugar
- 2 oz Bourbon or Rye
- (Scotch Whiskey in the London Sour Cocktail)

The recipe of the Eastern Sour Cocktail is, in my opinion, one of the best and innovative of Trader Vic. It is now well established that Tiki mixing was born with the exclusive use of rum. But, if Donn Beach has the merit of inventing the exotic cocktail, it will be instead merit of Trader Vic to lengthen the longevity of what is uniformly considered Tiki mixing.

Technique:

Shake and Pour with crushed ice

Service and Decoration

Low tumbler like Mai Tai Cocktail, mint, pineapple and cherry decoration

Tips

I highly recommend using a home made horchata. Only in this case to substitute HM orzata (less pungent than industrial) for the sugar. You can use a total of 3/4 oz of home made orzata.

NAVY GROG COCKTAIL

July 31, 1970, one of the most important dates of the maritime alcoholic tradition and of the whole history of mixing. On this day, called Black Tot Day, the Royal Navy definitively ceased the distribution of the daily ration, the "tot", of the mythical navy Grog. The imposition of Admiral Edward Vernon, who decided to lengthen with four parts of water the powerful distillates served on board in order to contrast the drunkenness of sailors, was born in 1740 and died on this historic day, July 31.

INGREDIENTS

- ¾ oz lime juice
- ¾ oz grapefruit juice
- ¾ oz soda
- 1 oz honey mix
- 1 oz puertorican rum
- 1 oz dark Jamaican rum
- 1 oz demerara rum

Technique:

- Recommended: Milkshake Mixer with 3 oz of ice
- Alternative: Shake and Strain

Decoration: ICE CONE

Service: LOW TUMBLER

Technique tip: omit the soda

DON'S SPECIAL DAIQUIRI

The popularity of this cocktail is attributable to the revaluation of the same in modern mixing. Today in fact it probably represents the easiest way to approach a structured and powerful mixing, at the same time refined, such as Donn's one. In this drink the predominance of Jamaican rum is attenuated in its fullness by the ruffling notes of honey and, at the same time, is exalted in its aromatic charge by the acidity of passion fruit syrup and lime.

INGREDIENTS

- 1 oz Gold Jamaican Rum
- 1/2 oz Puerto Rican Rum
- 1/2 oz Passion Fruit Syrup

- 1/2 oz Honey Syrup
- 1/2 oz Lime Juice

Technique: Milkshake mixer

Service: Cocktail glass.

Technical Tips

Unlike most of the cocktails of the first tiki era, Don's Special Daiquiri is a drink in which the technique in my opinion can also vary according to the ingredients used. My belief remains in any case that the best result is obtained by mixing the drink with a milkshake mixer.

However, in case we use rums which are not particularly aged, not too aromatic and not too full bodied, it is possible to obtain excellent results with the Shake and Strain technique.

SCORPION COCKTAIL

The Scorpion is one of Trader Vic's most well-known drinks. A cocktail that perfectly represents the new style in which Vic transports the era of exotic mixing after the 50's. A drink in which acidity and freshness hide the alcoholic charge of an original blend of spirits. The Scorpion recipe and the Scorpion Bowl itself, will be among the most imitated recipes and tiki mugs of the Tiki era.

INGREDIENTS

- 4 oz Fresh Lemon Juice
- 6 oz Fresh Orange Juice
- 1 1/2 oz Barley water
- 6 oz Spanish-style light rum (preferably amber)
- 1 oz Brandy

Technique: Blended for a few seconds with crushed ice (shake and pour in the single version)

Serving: Serve for 3 or 4 people in the Scorpion Bowl

Decoration: Mint and flowers (orchid or gardenia)

FORBIDDEN MAI TAI

Forbidden Mai Tai with hazelnut syrup made from hazelnut flour. This Forbidden Mai Tai was created precisely to differentiate the way rum is drunk in cocktails. In fact, as it should be in every Mai Tai, the blend of rums will be the main actor of the drink. But let's see the recipe of Forbidden Mai Tai right now.

INGREDIENTS

- 3/4 oz Lemon Hazelnut Syrup
- 1 oz Lime Juice
- 1/2 oz dry Curacao
- 1 3/4 oz Santa Teresa 1796 rum
- 3/4 oz Wray & Nephew rum

Technique: Shake and Pour with crushed ice.

Serving: Low tumbler, no straw.

Decoration: Mint tuft in the center and spiral of orange peel.

THE AUTHENTIC MAI TAI

The Mai Tai is a classic tiki cocktail that was invented in the 1940s by Victor Bergeron, the founder of Trader Vic's restaurant. It's a refreshing blend of rum, citrus, and almond flavors that's perfect for sipping on a hot summer day.

INGREDIENTS:

- 2 oz. dark rum
- 1 oz. fresh lime juice
- 1/2 oz. orange curaçao
- 1/2 oz. orgeat syrup
- Mint sprig, for garnish

INSTRUCTIONS:

1. Fill a shaker with ice.
2. Add the dark rum, fresh lime juice, orange curaçao, and orgeat syrup to the shaker.
3. Shake vigorously for about 15 seconds.
4. Strain the mixture into a glass filled with crushed ice.
5. Garnish with a mint sprig.

ZOMBIE

The Zombie is a tiki cocktail that was invented by Donn Beach in the 1930s. It's a potent blend of rum, fruit juices, and spices that's perfect for those who like their cocktails on the stronger side.

INGREDIENTS:

- 1 oz. white rum
- 1 oz. golden rum
- 1 oz. dark rum
- 1 oz. lime juice
- 1 oz. pineapple juice
- 1/2 oz. grenadine
- 1/2 oz. apricot brandy
- 1/2 oz. 151 proof rum
- Pineapple wedge and cherry, for garnish

INSTRUCTIONS:

1. Fill a shaker with ice.
2. Add the white rum, golden rum, dark rum, lime juice, pineapple juice, grenadine, and apricot brandy to the shaker.
3. Shake vigorously for about 15 seconds.
4. Strain the mixture into a glass filled with crushed ice.
5. Float the 151 proof rum on top of the cocktail.
6. Garnish with a pineapple wedge and cherry.

SWEET PAINKILLER

The Painkiller is a classic tiki cocktail that was invented in the British Virgin Islands in the 1970s. It's a creamy blend of rum, pineapple, orange, and coconut flavors that's perfect for sipping on a hot summer day.

INGREDIENTS:

- 2 oz. dark rum
- 4 oz. pineapple juice
- 1 oz. orange juice
- 1 oz. coconut cream
- Nutmeg, for garnish

INSTRUCTIONS:

1. Fill a shaker with ice.
2. Add the dark rum, pineapple juice, orange juice, and coconut cream to the shaker.
3. Shake vigorously for about 15 seconds.
4. Strain the mixture into a glass filled with ice.
5. Garnish with freshly grated nutmeg.

BLUE HAWAIIAN

The Blue Hawaiian is a popular tiki cocktail that's a twist on the classic Piña Colada. It's a bright blue cocktail that's both refreshing and fruity.

INGREDIENTS:

- 1 oz. light rum
- 1 oz. blue curaçao
- 2 oz. pineapple juice
- 1 oz. cream of coconut
- Pineapple wedge and cherry, for garnish

INSTRUCTIONS:

1. Fill a shaker with ice.
2. Add the light rum, blue curaçao, pineapple juice, and cream of coconut to the shaker.
3. Shake vigorously for about 15 seconds.
4. Strain the mixture into a glass filled with ice.
5. Garnish with a pineapple wedge and cherry.

BAHAMA MAMA

The Bahama Mama is a tropical tiki cocktail that's perfect for sipping on the beach. It's a fruity blend of rum, pineapple, orange, and coconut flavors.

INGREDIENTS:

- 1 oz. light rum
- 1 oz. dark rum
- 1 oz. coconut rum
- 2 oz. pineapple juice
- 2 oz. orange juice
- 1 oz. cream of coconut
- Pineapple wedge and cherry, for garnish

INSTRUCTIONS:

1. Fill a shaker with ice.
2. Add the light rum, dark rum, coconut rum, pineapple juice, orange juice, and cream of coconut to the shaker.

3. Shake vigorously for about 15 seconds.

4. Strain the mixture into a glass filled with ice.

5. Garnish with a pineapple wedge and cherry.

Printed in Great Britain
by Amazon